T0147545

Journey of the Mind, Journey of the Soul

The Key to Holistic Well-Being and Happiness

Dr. Michael H. Likey, Ph.D., D.D.

iUniverse, Inc.

New York Bloomington

Journey of the Mind, Journey of the Soul
The Key to Holistic Well-Being and Happiness

Copyright © 2009 by Dr. Michael H. Likey, Ph.D., D.D.

All rights reserved. No part of this book may be used or reproduced by any means, graphic, electronic, or mechanical, including photocopying, recording, taping or by any information storage retrieval system without the written permission of the publisher except in the case of brief quotations embodied in critical articles and reviews.

iUniverse books may be ordered through booksellers or by contacting:

iUniverse
1663 Liberty Drive
Bloomington, IN 47403
www.iuniverse.com
1-800-Authors (1-800-288-4677)

Because of the dynamic nature of the Internet, any Web addresses or links contained in this book may have changed since publication and may no longer be valid. The views expressed in this work are solely those of the author and do not necessarily reflect the views of the publisher, and the publisher hereby disclaims any responsibility for them.

ISBN: 978-1-4401-3107-3 (pbk)
ISBN: 978-1-4401-3106-6 (ebk)

Printed in the United States of America

iUniverse rev. date: 3/25/2009

Journey of the Mind, Journey of the Soul

Contents

Part 2 — God: Religion, Theology, Philosophy, Spirituality, and Metaphysics

Acknowledgements

My thanks and deep appreciation goes to everyone who is on this path of enlightenment, and to all of you who seek to uncover the great truths.

A special thanks to my parents (deceased) for believing in me.

I must give thanks, as well, to iUniverse and to all of its helpful employees, without whom this book would not have seen the light of day.

Thanks to you all.

Preface
By Dr. Michael Likey

As a Doctor of Metaphysical Science, I am responsible for the spiritual guidance of my clients, patients and students. Some seek me out for answers to regular, day-to-day issues. Others seek me out for answers to larger questions such as "Why am I here?" or "What is my soul's purpose?" To assist those clients with those questions, I, as a certified Clinical Hypnotherapist, usually hypnotically regress them, so that they may understand what previous lifetime karmic-activity might be relevant to this lifetime; this usually helps them to understand why they are like the way they are in this life.

I am a great promoter for my students and clients, of their own independence and self-empowerment, by them going inward, that is to say, meditating for the purposes of contacting the Divine, Higher Consciousness, Creator, Source-Energy, God, etc. for their own answers.

It is because I am a Clinical Hypnotherapist, Doctor of Metaphysical Science, and Ordained Metaphysical Minister, do metaphysical/spiritual counseling, Reiki/energy-healing, head up my own metaphysical ministry, and have helped thousands of clients, patients and students to "evolve" spiritually, that I feel qualified to write this book.

Because I have conducted years of research into the effects and benefits of various kinds of meditations, conducted hundreds of hours of guided meditations, hypnosis, and performed dozens of Mind-Treatments (which we now call "Alpha Quantum Therapy" ©) that I am qualified to write this book, in addition to my educational background, which included metaphysics, philosophy, psychology, to name just a few.

Enjoy reading this labor of love, which I trust will enlighten you, and add to the quality of your life, and the lives of others.

Introduction

Defining Metaphysics

According to Herman J. Aaftink, the Founder-Director of the Calgary Life Enrichment Centre, and Author of "Brand New Me-The Art of Authentic Living", "Metaphysics" is the popular name for the ancient philosophy of Idealism, first taught by Plato and Aristotle about 2,500 years ago. Metaphysics means "beyond physics": it is the attempt to present a comprehensive, coherent and consistent account of reality, of the Universe as a whole, including ourselves. Metaphysics is also referred to as a branch of Philosophy that deals with First Cause and the Nature of Being. It is taught as a branch of Philosophy in most academic universities today under the label of "Speculative Philosophy." According to Aaftink, "Metaphysics acknowledges a "cosmic", or "Universal mind" (or "God-Mind") as the operating principle of order and change as well as the source of all existence".

Dr. Paul Leon Masters, the Founder/CEO of the two oldest and most respected Universities of Metaphysics in the world, the "University of Metaphysics", and the "University of Sedona", both being two of my Alma Maters, states "the word "Metaphysics" has become a description of many fields of interest. When one expresses an interest in Metaphysics, that interest may be in any one or a combination of the following subjects: Philosophy, Religion, Parapsychology, Mysticism, Yoga, ESP, Dreams, Jungian Psychology, Astrology, Meditation, Self-Help Studies, Positive Thinking, Life After Death, Reincarnation, etc. The common denominator of these and all similar subjects deals with an exploration of Reality, and in the idealistic sense, how such knowledge may benefit human life on this earth, both individually and collectively". According to Masters, "if, then, this is the aim of such interests, it is why most professional Metaphysical Practitioners (that is to say, Practitioners of Metaphysical Counseling and Healing) regard Metaphysics as a Spiritual Philosophy of life. All but a very few practitioners in Metaphysics today have a pivotal point of some sort of Spiritual Philosophy in whatever system or teaching of Metaphysics they are engaged. If we were to travel from one metaphysical teacher or organization to another", he goes on to say, "we would find people engaging in different things, all under the label of Metaphysics. This could be a wide range, such as yogis, mystics, astrologers, positive thinking teachers, meditation teachers, grapho-analysts, spiritual healers, self-help teachers, etc. The range is wide, but again the basic denominator is the search for truth, purpose and meaning in life, which cannot be isolated from basic spiritual questions".

The basis for most of these beliefs/perspectives come not only from the ancient Greek philosophers, but also the Hindu mystics, ancient mystical/esoteric Buddhist teachings, and even the Taoist "Immortals" who created the now-popular Qi Gong, Tai Chi, and Kung (or Gong) Fu practices of meditative breathing and gentle physical exercises for health and longevity, in China. Swami Vivekananda, a Hindu mystic who lived from 1863-1902 is considered to be largely responsible for bringing Yoga, again, a series of deep-breathing exercises and poses as a means to maintaining and increasing health and longevity, to Europe and to America, while the Maharishi Mahesh Yogi, another Indian mystic made popular by the Beatles in the 1960's, is considered responsible for bringing "Mystical Meditation", whose purpose is Divine-contact, healing, and health-maintenance, (as opposed to "Western" or "Guided Meditations" which are mainly for relaxation, and for eliminating unwanted behaviors/habits) to the west.

I will be referring to "Metaphysics" from the perspective of the practice of "Western" or "Guided Meditation" and self-hypnosis, mainly, within this book, as the basis for health. Again, you may look at this as essentially using the relatively untapped potential, or "power" of the human mind, with self-hypnosis or meditation being the key to tapping, exploring, and/or opening it. Therefore, one of the main aims of this book is not so much working with metaphysics from a "speculative-philosophical/spiritual" perspective, but more from a practical and clinical perspective, and thereby supplying to the reader potential tools for healing and health-maintenance through the power of the mind.

Science has already for many years measured and acknowledged health gains as a result of the practice of Western Meditation and self-hypnosis for, among other things, stress-management, (which encourages greater psychological "peace-of-mind") reduced high blood-pressure, increased physical stamina, etc.

The benefits of meditation and self-hypnosis has long been scientifically acknowledged in the treatment of weight-loss, improving self-esteem, stopping/discouraging unwanted habits such as smoking, etc.

I will be outlining some of my own research results/experiences with my various clients as a Clinical Hypnotherapist and Doctor of Metaphysical Science, to further underline the points I will be making within this book.

We will not so much be discussing self-hypnosis/meditation as a means for Divine-contact, only because any sort of actual "Divine-contact" via meditation/self-hypnosis/yoga, etc. has yet to be proven clinically. This being said, however, results from ongoing scientifically-measured and monitored praying and meditating nuns in Quebec, Canada, in recent years, has shown an increase in activity in a specific part of the human-brain. This seems to indicate a kind of physiological reaction in the brain to religious-prayer and Mystical Meditation, but not much else.

Metaphysics as a spiritual way of life will also not be discussed in this book either, although contemporary spiritual movements such as "Christian Science" (founded by Mary Baker Eddy, a former patient who was "cured" by P.P. Quimby), "Religious Science", or "Science of Mind" (founded by Ernest Holmes) and "Unity", also grew out of Phineas Parkhurst Quimby's practice and studies of the 1850's.

Metaphysics for Health

The more "practical" application of Metaphysics as a means to better health and healing was rediscovered by the aforementioned Phineas Parkhurst Quimby on the east-coast of 19th century America, via his study of "mesmerism" (or hypnosis), which in turn became the basis of modern-day Clinical Hypnotherapy and Psychotherapy, including "Transpersonal Psychology". Self-hypnosis was later employed by the famous therapist Sigmund Freud on his patients, who, along with Carl Jung, (metaphysician and therapist) also analyzed patients' dreams as a means of understanding their unconscious mind, wherein theoretically was stored the basis to ill-mental, emotional (and in Quimby's belief-system, physical) health. The manner in which Quimby employed a combination of psychology, theology, intuition, and mild hypnosis and meditation, was also the basis for "NLP", or "Neuro-Linguistic Programming", a now-popular form of psychotherapy made popular by Milton Erikson, in addition to contributing to Beck's creation of "Cognitive Therapy". We will discuss in detail later Quimby's methodologies, comparing them in practical terms to some contemporary therapeutic clinical methodologies, my own clinical use of all methods, as well as how the reader may practically employ some of these methods for improving and maintaining health.

Qualifications

What qualifies me to write this book?

Among other things, as started earlier, I am a certified and qualified Doctor of Metaphysics, (with a double-Doctorate: a Ph.D. in Mystical Research from the University of Sedona, and a Doctor of Divinity from the University of Metaphysics) Ordained Metaphysical Minister, and Clinical Hypnotherapist. This means that using my learned knowledge of Holmes' philosophies, Quimby's "New Thought" techniques of mesmerism, Mind/Metaphysical/ Meditative Treatments, conventional Clinical Hypnotherapy techniques, (rooted, as previously stated, in Quimby's "New Thought" practices, in any case) and Metaphysical and Western Psychology. (which, as also stated, are based in the ancient wisdom and philosophies of the sages, plus Quimby, Jung, Freud, and the other contemporary therapists)

My intense education and experience in Hypnotherapy was gained through the Robert Shields College of Hypnotherapy, England. I am an Associate-Member of the Canadian International Metaphysical Ministry, member of the American Metaphysical Doctors Association, and member of the Association of Ethical and Professional Hypnotherapists. (England)

I have also counseled Pastorally/Spiritually/Metaphysically thousands of patients and clients. What that means is that I provided information, resources, and tools, all "God"-based. Whatever the person's definition/ concept of "God" was is what I worked with; I have not yet, in my 15 years out of a total of 30 in the field of Metaphysics, as a Metaphysical Counselor, encountered anyone who had no belief in God, or some sort of a Higher, creative power. This is probably due to the very nature of the field I am in. Also, because I believed intuitively, as I still do, that we have all the answers stored somewhere deep within us, and I have always tried/try to guide the person to finding the solutions themselves, rather than depend on some outside source, be it another person, etc., thus they are truly self-empowered. Certainly I would be fooling myself and be less than truthful to you, if I denied my highly-developed sense of intuition, which always guided me to ask the "right" questions of the patients and clients in a session, thereby leading them to emotional breakthroughs, which healthier, happier lifestyle is based upon. This "intuition" I cannot and will not try to explain scientifically, but more "philosophically": it is "God-given". I cannot deny, that like the aforementioned P.P. Quimby, I could almost always, with more than ninety-percent accuracy, pinpoint what was troubling them on the inside, without them initially stating their issue(s) and with sixty to seventy-percent accuracy, pinpoint the emotional causes of their unhappiness; further probing and questioning would determine/confirm the usual childhood/adolescent/early adult traumatic reasons for their distress. Hypnosis and/or meditative treatments and techniques with "God the Healer" being the basis, thus far, has resulted in an eighty-to-ninety-percent "success" rate, or "healing" of past emotional traumas of my clients, as opposed to the more contemporary and commercially-accepted Clinical Hypnotherapy techniques. This is what qualifies me to write this book.

As a Clinical Hypnotherapist for a number of years, I have initiated self-hypnosis to assist my patients in improving their self-esteem, controlling their weight, and to stop smoking, among other things. These patients have reported a more than eighty-percent success-rate to me.

As a Doctor of Metaphysical Science, I have been also utilizing meditation in a similar fashion, because: (a) The Alpha brainwave state in self-hypnosis is identical to the brainwave-state during meditation, (Shields, 1986) and: (b) At the request of some clients, whom, for one reason or another preferred meditation over self-hypnosis. These same clients have also been reporting a similar success-rate to me as well, in the improvement of their self-esteem and for controlling their weight.

I have also been facilitating during this same year, regular weekly "Mystical Meditations", the goal being for my students, clients, and patients to experience contact with the Divine within them, and also for eliminating their unwanted thought-patterns (Masters, 1989), for example, thoughts and feelings of lack, as opposed to thoughts and feelings of abundance and prosperity.

In addition to these regular meditation gatherings, I have also been, during this past year facilitating weekly "Chakral Meditations", based on the works of myself, Dr. Masters, and Dr. Mishra's book "Fundamentals of Yoga", re-published in 1987. The purpose of this meditation being purely observational: during this "Yogic-Meditation", in which the students focus upon each of the energy-centers, or "Chakras" of their bodies, what occurs in their minds? Do they seem to reap any concrete rewards/results? Are these results/rewards purely metaphysical, clinical, or a combination?

What I partially intend to explore in the context of this book are the results of these two meditational groups, in order to outline the workings of the human brain, and more specifically, the human mind; how emotions created by memories rooted deep within the memory-banks of the brain, or mind, affect the day-to-day quality of our life, including goal-setting and health. Comparisons of meditation and hypnosis will follow, as will theological, psychological, philosophical, and metaphysical perspectives and discussions on the implications of defining the existence of God deep within the human brain or mind, and finally how this "God-Power" may be harnessed to encourage optimum health overall.

Initially, I intend to discuss the experiences and responses of my meditation students, based on the practical research I have done through questions, answers, and discussions with the two separate meditation groups over the last year: what are their experiences (visual, auditory, etc.)? Do they feel/believe they have/are achieving union with the Divine, and if so, why do they believe this? For example, what are the experiences? What other things do the students feel that they are achieving through meditation? How is this manifesting? For example, relaxation, evolution of their soul, progress in their day-to-day lives, etc. Is their intuition (or Divine-guidance) increasing, thereby placing them in a "Divine-Flow" of their soul's purpose/synchronicity of life-events, etc.? How is this being proven to them? Has the quality of their life overall improved, and if so, in what ways? Do they believe that they are having any paranormal/psychic experiences during meditation, and if so, what are those experiences? For example, experiencing past-lives, angels, guides, etc. How do they feel about these paranormal experiences?

Are my students succeeding in the concrete or clinical realm/arena, such as in weight-loss, improved self-esteem, etc.?

Next, what will follow will be a discussion of these answers, and their implications: How useful from a Clinical Therapist's perspective have these experiences been?

How useful from a Metaphysician's perspective, for example, in professional use as a Doctor of Metaphysics, have these experiences been?

As stated earlier, I will ultimately describe the various processes which have improved the quality of my patients' and clients' lives. They are all happier and healthier on all levels. My recent use of "Mind-Treatments", loosely based on Quimby's techniques, and not dissimilar to the aforementioned treatments, have further increased the percentile of healed patients!

Thus, in writing this book, I intend to emphasize for other Metaphysicians and Clinical Hypnotherapists, as well as for the broad public, the importance/benefits of meditation from a clinical, as well as spiritual/metaphysical perspective, as well as how these finding may affect society as a whole.

PART 1-

THE HUMAN BRAIN: A PRIMER

▼

CHAPTER I

The Organ

We will not define the human brain right now, in detailed, scientific, and biological terms. We will discuss in detail further on in this book the brain as a processor of perceptions.

At this point, we choose to refer to the human brain as the computer of the human body. It is that which stores up memories and events that have occurred in the person's physical environment. It is not necessary that we describe how the brain processes the physical senses such as sight, smell, etc., nor do we deem it relevant that we describe the processes of the brain which allows such things as motor-skill movement. In the words of Swami Vivekananda in Volume 6 of "The Complete Works of Swami Vivekananda", he states, "The Ophthamalic Centre in the brain is the organ of sight, not the eye alone...only when the mind reacts, is the object truly perceived." In other words, it is enough that the brain is the true processor, or computer, if you will, of that which our human senses perceive; it is our brain that rights the inverted-images that our eyes see; it is our human-mind that subjectively perceives an event in our life to be positive or negative; it is our memory-bank, or "Personal Subconscious" part of our brain that stores events that occur in our life, and what Jung called the "Collective Unconscious" part of our mind that transforms people formerly and currently in our lives into mythological-like "gods" or "goddesses": good or evil characters on an unconscious-level, based on, again, the human-mind part of our brain.

All that we will concern ourselves within the context of this book, is firstly the brain's function as it is relevant to memory, and perceptions of memory, and secondly, the duality of the human brain in regards to creative and emotional function versus the reasoning, logical part of the brain.

Science has already proven that one half of the human brain processes logic and reason, while the other hemisphere concerns itself with the function of creativity and emotions.

Recent scientific research in Wisconsin has also determined that the stress hormones produced within the brains of monkeys have been proven to be the cause of the emotions of fear and anxiety.

Getting to the Sources of Fear and Anxiety

Wisconsin emotion researchers have been studying defensive behaviors in monkeys to better understand the related temperament that may put humans at risk, including extreme shyness, excessive anxiety and exaggerated fearfulness. The researchers have found that chronically fearful and anxious monkeys have specific patterns of brain electrical activity as well as elevated levels of two kinds of stress hormones. Their latest study challenges the existing theory that the brain structure called the amygdala controls all fear and anxiety responses. The findings show that in primates, the amygdala is involved in acute fear responses, but doesn't appear to play a role in anxiety responses that may be present from early in life and related to general temperament.

Brain Responses to Antidepressants

A new drug called venlafaxine is proving to be very successful clinically in treating depression, but how exactly does it affect brain function? This study uses functional magnetic resonance imaging (FMRI) techniques to establish how antidepressants such as venlafaxine can reverse the brain alterations that are associated with depression. The study also explores how treatment with medications may change depressed patients' responses to positive and negative stimuli.

Fearful Temperament Points to Vulnerability

The free-ranging male monkeys of Cayo Santiago, a small island off Puerto Rico, provide a unique opportunity to study biological factors associated with different kinds of emotional and social styles because they normally go through a highly stressful event during adolescence that results in death for 25 percent of them. UW researchers have identified monkeys for whom this process is especially difficult and have found that the animals have fearful temperaments as well as specific brain activity and hormone levels related to elevated stress. Additional physiological measures will be taken to learn which constellation of factors may make some monkeys more vulnerable to stress and more susceptible to disease than others.

Meditation and the Brain

In this small but highly provocative study, the UW-Madison research team also found for the first time, in humans, that a short program in "mindfulness meditation" produced lasting positive changes in both the human brain and the function of the immune system.

The findings suggest that meditation, long promoted as a technique to reduce anxiety and stress, might produce important biological effects that improve a person's resiliency.

Richard Davidson, Vilas Professor of psychology and psychiatry at UW-Madison, led the research team. The study, conducted at the biotechnology company Promega near Madison, will appeared in the Journal Psychosomatic Medicine.

"Mindfulness meditation," often recommended as an antidote to the stress and pain of chronic disease, is a practice designed to focus one's attention intensely on the moment, noting thoughts and feelings as they occur but refraining from judging or acting on those thoughts and feelings. The intent is to deepen awareness of the present, develop skills of focused attention, and cultivate positive emotions such as compassion.

In the UW study, participants were randomly assigned to one of two groups. The experimental group, with 25 subjects, received training in mindfulness meditation from one of its most noted adherents, Jon Kabat-Zinn, (Kabat-Zinn, a popular author of books on stress reduction, developed the mindfulness-based stress reduction program at the University of Massachusetts Medical Center.) This group attended a weekly class and one seven-hour retreat during the study; they also were assigned home practice for an hour a day, six days a week. The 16 members of the control group did not receive meditation training until after the study was completed.

For each group, in addition to asking the participants to assess how they felt, the research team measured electrical activity in the frontal part of the brain, an area specialized for certain kinds of emotion. Earlier research has shown that, in people who are generally positive and optimistic and during times of positive emotion, the left side of this frontal area becomes more active than the right side does.

The findings confirmed the researchers' hypothesis: the meditation group showed an increase of activation in the left-side part of the frontal region. This suggests that the meditation itself produced more activity in this region of the brain. This activity is associated with lower anxiety and a more positive emotional state.

The research team also tested whether the meditation group had better immune function than the control group did. All the study participants got a flu vaccine at the end of the eight-week meditation group. Then, at four and eight weeks after vaccine administration, both groups had blood tests to measure the level of antibodies they had produced against the flu vaccine. While both groups (as expected) had developed increased antibodies, the meditation group had a significantly larger increase than the controls, at both four and eight weeks after receiving the vaccine.

"Although our study is preliminary and more research clearly is warranted," said Davidson, "we are very encouraged by these results. The Promega employees who took part have given us a wonderful opportunity to demonstrate a real biological impact of this ancient practice."

Davidson, who is integrally involved with the Health Emotions Research Institute at UW, plans further research on the impact of meditation. He is currently studying a group of people who have been using meditation for more than 30 years. His research team is also planning to study the impact of mindfulness meditation on patients with particular illnesses.

My Own Research

Following is information based on feedback received from my students of meditation over the course of a year. Their names and specifics were altered to allow for their anonymity.

Allan is a forty-something male in the entertainment industry, who until a year ago, had little previous experience with meditation and spirituality. I informally met him one day through a workshop a colleague of mine was facilitating. Allan's motivation for joining both of our newly-formed Mystical Meditation, and Chakral Meditation groups, was to "open" his third-eye; in his words, to "Develop latent Psychic abilities." I sensed initially that he was a natural-born healer, that is to say, with God's help he could initiate the self-healing of others. I told him this, and I also referred to him as an "Earth Angel", which he seemed to resonate to. I use this term "Earth Angel" solely because it seems to intuitively "open" people up to understanding the idea of "being there for others", for a "greater purpose", or "service". My motivation with Allan was to help him to see that "psychic abilities/paranormal experiences" are merely a rung along the step up the ladder to being one with God (Masters, 1989); that union/contact with the Divine within us should be the primary goal, with everything else being secondary. I let him know this, just to be clear as to my own motives. He agreed to participate.

This meeting of Allan coincided with the time I e-mailed an invitation to the Mystical and Chakral Meditation-nights at our home, to my existing clients, patients, and students. Our rather large living-room comfortably accommodates twelve people, so I wasn't worried about how many would attend.

Immediately after this e-mail invitation was sent out, Ellen, a 22-year-old unemployed female, expressed interest in attending, as well as Lucy, a forty-something Legal Secretary, both of whom were patients of mine. I felt that these individuals were relatively diverse in education and background, had no previous formal experience in meditation or self-hypnosis, and that it would be interesting to hear what their feedback was with this meditation. What they all shared was a decided interest in matters Metaphysical: Ellen was reading many popular self-help books, and Lucy had experienced some paranormal activity, specifically those with spirits and ghosts allegedly, in the home she shared with her husband. She also wished to do healings with animals, which was what motivated her to be my Reiki-student, as well. She also had a profound faith in God. Allan was the Reiki-student of that colleague of mine, who referred him to me.

The first evening of our weekly Mystical Meditation night, I made it clear that the primary purpose was Union with the Divine, and secondly, to re-program any unwanted/negative thought-patterns, eventually replacing them with prosperity, health, and abundance. Anything extra gained/ experienced during these nights was a bonus, I added, and that at the very least, it was their "quality" time of feeling peace and relaxation from their busy day/week. I asked them to not expect anything concrete or specific. Just to enjoy. Then, I asked them to close their eyes, and imagine that they are looking up and into the centre of their brain, where their Pineal-gland resides; The Pineal gland (also called the Pineal Body, Epiphysis Cerebri, or Third-Eye) is a small <u>endocrine</u> gland in the vertebrate <u>brain</u>. It produces <u>melatonin</u>, a hormone that affects the modulation of wake/sleep patterns and photoperiodic (seasonal) functions. (Wikipedia 2008) I sometimes refer to this as the "interior-region of their head", rather than the "brain", as it sounds less clinical. Traditionally, though, during Yogic/Kundalini-Meditation, one of the major "energy-centers" or "Chakras" is traditionally referred-to as the "brain". (Mishra, 1987) The basic, clinical concept being that when one attempts to stimulate their Pineal gland, using whatever method, that hormonal-secretions created by this, stimulates a series of sensations which may be interpreted as "spiritual" or Metaphysical". These "experiences" are often linked with union with the Higher Self/God/God-Mind.

It is the not the purpose/goal of this book to debate the validity of this.

Further, it has been noted, from a clinical perspective, that focusing up and slightly back, (towards the brow-area) with or without eyes opened or closed, induces a light-meditative state. (Shields, 1986) This is sometimes why, as Hypnotherapists, we ask the subject to focus (with their eyes open) up and back towards a spot on the ceiling, or on the tip of a pencil/pendulum/pocket-watch, etc. held over their heads: after a minute or so, their eyelids do become heavier, as their eyes strain back to focus on that point.

The three attendees were then asked to sit with their backs straight, (to facilitate the flow of Kundalini-energy; clinically, to enable an easier, deeper breathing) and with either their feet planted firmly on the ground or their ankles crossed, (which ever felt more comfortable) to simply "relax" and "let go".

I clicked on the meditation-music, and began reading from my script. Technically-speaking, the first ten-minutes is an "induction" (Shields, 1986), or script designed to take them to "Alpha" or meditative/daydream brainwave-state, perfect for relaxation and therapeutic-uses such as re-programming unwanted thought-patterns (Goldberg, 1998). In my Hypnotherapy practice, I have a tendency of taking my patients to a deeper "Theta" (or near-sleep) brainwave-state, useful for Soul-Regression (Goldberg, 1998) and Past-Life Regressions, so I felt somewhat insecure about guiding them only to Alpha, fearing that it wouldn't yield any results. I quickly remembered how incredible my own personal meditative experiences in Alpha-state have been for almost thirty years, so this then calmed any concerns I had. The next twenty-minutes consisted of some of the affirmative meditations for re-programming unwanted thought-patterns, which I had studied in my Ministers/Bachelors program from Dr. Masters' course, (Masters, 1989) and the last five minutes was from a script designed to "bring them back" up and out from "Alpha" to wide-awake state, or "Beta"-state. (Hewitt, 1997)

The feedback that followed this initial meditation greatly surprised me.

Allan described a purple light in front of him, and a feeling of heat and vibrations in his hands which he attributed to the flow of the healing-energy known as "Reiki". Lucy described the identical experience, while Ellen went into a detailed account of having "seen" her "animal guides", describing a black panther and other large, protective cats that she had seen around her during the meditation. I asked her how this made her feel, and she said "good" and "protected". I let her know that these visions are from God, confirmations of His protection of us, but she insists, still to this day, that they are her "animal totem" or "animal guides". I feel that if this belief empowers people, it is not for me to argue/discredit them. Clinically, I believe they are archetypes we carry deep within our unconscious-mind, in other words, how we really see ourselves, and our strengths. Interpreted thusly, in her case, she unconsciously feels she has the strength, loyalty and tenacity of those big cats. The final result is the same, regardless: self-empowerment.

Over the next six months, all three attendees seemed to move forward in their individual lives: all attracting jobs/careers/love-lives that gratified them; Metaphysically, I attribute this to the Divine-contact accomplished during meditation, which allowed them to, among other things: (a) Open a channel to becoming more Intuitive, or God-guided day-to-day, thereby allowing them to be at the right place, at the right time, with the right person(s) for the receiving/initiation of their prosperity (b) Improve their self-esteem, through these healing, meditative "Mind-Treatments", (Masters, 1989) thus allowing them to make changes in their lives with greater courage, confidence, and conviction, and (c) By being more God-guided, they were living more and more their "soul's purpose(s)", that is to say evolving more in a positive, healthful way, to be more and more of "service" to others and to themselves. Clinically, I attribute this to the attendees gaining greater self-esteem and confidence through the suggestions made during the self-hypnotic/meditative-state. (That they are stronger, healed, happier, etc.) They are more prone to hang onto these suggestions subliminally, in their subconscious mind, via the suggestions given under hypnotic-state.

Lucy, for example, almost a year later, is now making a great deal of money in her spare time doing Reiki on animals, so much so, that this income may soon replace her full-time Legal Secretary position! She is richer financially as well as emotionally and spiritually. She attributes this to the Divine-contact made during the Mystical Meditations.

Allan has a clearer vision of what he wants to do: he has been acquiring more alternative-wellness modalities, with the hopes of eventually leaving his full-time job and starting a wellness centre. He too attributes this to a "oneness" with God he feels and experiences during this meditation.

Ellen appears to be more "employable" in the material-world, supplementing her government check with part-time, non-metaphysically-related work, and is happier and emotionally healthier. She believes that this is due with the contact with God she has during the Mystical Meditations.

Overall, they seem to have a stronger base of God, and are far more confident.

In this almost twelve-month process, they have also been experiencing much more, during the Mystical Meditation nights, which by the way, now consists of as little as five, and as many as ten people regularly attending on the Wednesday-nights!

Ellen's experiences seem more elaborate, consisting of "journeys" to places she describes in detail, usually "floating" over, around and through these places in her visions. Many times, she is "underwater", with a dolphin as a guide, other times she "sees" multi-colored fields with fountains and/or mountains, her black-panther guiding her all the way. She has seen people she recognizes from this lifetime, understanding the purposes for them being in her life now.

The therapeutic aspect of meditation for her is undeniable, far quicker, and less expensive than if I would hypnotically regress her to these "past-lives".

This would suggest that meditation definitely has therapeutic benefits, as well as potentially being a substitute in many cases for hypnosis.

Allan's experiences, although less dramatic on the Wednesday, or Mystical Meditation nights, are if anything, consistent. He continues seeing light, either purple or green, symbolically representing to him healing and protection around him, as he has expressed.

Lucy often sees either what she perceives as "angels", and/or souls from previous lives. I've explained to her that our soul carries past-memories from previous lives in its Astral-Body (Masters, 1989) and meditation opens up a channel, enables her to "see" and/or remember these souls. Clinically, although I've also explained to her that the "angels" and "guides" are unconscious extensions of the strengths she carries of herself in her unconscious-mind, which are also physical manifestations of God, she prefers believing that these are actual angels and guides. She also claims to see her deceased mother around her, often times during meditation-periods. This makes her feel loved, protected, empowered, and hopeful. Who am I to argue with this? When she first began meditating, she did not have any of these experiences. Her desire to "grow spiritually and psychically" continues to be satisfied, apparently. From an emotional and psychological perspective, I believe this to be all positive. Her self-esteem has grown ten-fold, compared to when she first started, showing me that the re-programming-to-abundance aspect works, and is just as effective for self-esteem issues as is self-hypnosis is, in my private practice. She has gained the confidence to approach strangers/potential clients and customers for her animal-healing business. From a spiritual, as well as psychological perspective, the Mystical Meditation nights are definitely working, and are still growing.

The Thursday-night Chakral Meditations yield fascinating results as well.

I had originally written this guided meditation to encourage an activation of the energy-centres known as "Chakras" within the body, and then to document the results in my students. Many of the students from my Wednesday-nights participate, but we also have attending several who exclusively attend only the Thursday-nights, because they generally prefer the "feel" or "energy" of the Thursday-nights over the Wednesday-nights. I have given everyone a chance to experience both nights, and now we have a consistent attendance over both nights. Some attend both nights, others attend only one or the other for the reasons just outlined: the "feel".

I will now proceed to describe the experiences that Ellen, Allan, and Lucy have on the Thursday-nights, (which are significantly different from their Wednesday-night experiences) in addition to those experiences of Greg, Helen, and Janet on the Thursday-nights. Greg, Helen, and Janet have tried the Wednesday-nights, preferring the Thursday-nights, while Ellen, Allan, and Lucy attend both nights.

Greg is a twenty-two-year-old ad executive, who has studied Reiki with my colleague and teaches yoga at a local outlet. He is satisfied with the Reiki-modality and is seeking to expand his wellness business, which includes the selling and promotion of a multi-level marketing nutritious fruit-drink. He is confident and well-adjusted.

Helen is a housewife and Reiki-Practitioner, lacking confidence, but attending meditation to build her self-esteem; although she regularly attends Thursday-nights and my Sunday-morning Metaphysical service, she does on occasion attend Wednesday-nights. She is fascinated with the paranormal, but leans towards the mystical, spiritual, and healing-aspects of life.

Janet is a forty-something housewife, mother of two grown children, and book-keeper. Fascinated with the paranormal and highly intuitive, she originally approached me to attune her to Reiki, so that she could help others to self-heal. Having lost her father-in-law last year to cancer, she believes she feels his spirit around her. Her goal is to be able to see him and all spirits/ghosts, so that she might help the living with closure. This is her primary motivation for attending our Thursday-night Chakral Meditation, although time allowing, she also attends the very occasional Wednesday-night meditation, again, preferring the "energy" to Thursday-night's meditation. She believes her psychic abilities will improve through regular meditation. She is also a strong believer in God, so I need not emphasize meditation as a means to union with the Divine with her.

Much like the Mystical Meditation, there are three parts, consisting of the aforementioned "induction", middle-part, or focusing one-at-a-time on each energy-centre and resting in the experiences of each one, and finally concluding with the wrap-up/guiding back up and out to the external world once again. During the period of time that I have been conducting the Chakral Meditations, the results have been dramatic for all.

All see "other-worldly" places and people they do not recognize.

The experiences are always of a paranormal nature, as opposed to the Mystical Meditation's revelation/spiritual/God-oriented experiences of peace and tranquility.

They all claim to have had these experiences during the phase of the meditation when they are asked to focus either on their naval, and/or brow/ centre-of-their-brain area.

Both Greg and Lucy have seen very clearly an "eye" in front of them. During this experience, they have attempted to see into the iris-part, but this yielded little results, that area appearing clouded thus far. I told them that this is like a mirror into their soul, and when they are ready, they will begin to see clearer. Clinically-speaking, both Greg and Lucy are intellectually-driven, with a strong literary background; to them, the "eye" subconsciously represents a certain level of spiritual-evolution they unconsciously feel proud of, therefore the "eye" physically manifests to them as a symbol of this evolution. When they believe, deep-down, that they have evolved even more, spiritually, they will no doubt be able to "enter into the iris", and even begin having experiences from that perspective. I don't feel it is necessary to share with them, at this point, the clinical explanation, as psychologically it might squash their enthusiasm and confidence to delve deeper.

All parties still experience glimpses of what they believe are past lifetimes; they base this on the manner of dress of the characters they are seeing. They believe these characters/personalities they are seeing to be people they know now, and have known before, and will know again. I explained this metaphysically to them: during these Chakral Meditations, they, in their oneness with their Higher-Self/God, etc. are in the Eternal-Moment: past/ present/future all exist at the same time; I further explained that this is how "Psychics" operate, at least those Mystically (or God)-oriented: in slightly altered-state, they can access that divine/eternal-moment, where glimpses of the past/present/future reside, in order to share the information gleaned from this experience with their clients, or in other words, by giving them a "reading". This explanation seems/seemed to satisfy the attendees intellectually. I added that the "Sleeping Prophet", Edgar Cayce, claimed a similar theory: that Psychics, during meditation, can apparently access the unconscious desires of those they are reading for, since we are all in one Mind of God, and the one Mind of God resides within us as well; this is much like the then-popular New Thought beliefs that are now re-emerging as well. I also reiterate about Jung's theory of archetypes/visual metaphors of ourselves which reside in our unconscious-mind: could these people they glimpse during meditation represent various aspects/strengths/weaknesses of their own personality/ character, thus enabling them to self-analyze and improve? I encourage them to do this.

These visions of past-lives during the Chakral Meditation-nights by the participants generally fascinate, entertain, if not encourage them to return, time and time again; if this attendance and participation in meditation results in them enabling their spiritual oneness with the Divine, thus creating a more God-guided ability amongst them, then I, too, am satisfied, feeling that I am accomplishing a greater purpose.

All tend to also see angelic-like figures as well, giving detailed descriptions of hair-color, dress, sex, etc. Again, I refer to Jung's more clinical explanations for this, but I also ask those experiencing these angels, what and whom they feel they represent to them, to get them to self-analyze and improve themselves.

Ellen's journeys are far more detailed and elaborate on the Thursday-nights, however, they are also "case-book" Jungian experiences: unconscious metaphors for fears/concerns in her conscious day-to-day living, and I continue helping her with these observations at other times via metaphysical consultations.

Lucy still feels she sees her deceased mother-in-law. I never discourage her about this, as long as she feels empowered by these visions.

Helen and Janet feel vibrations in their hands and warmth which they believe to be Reiki, Helen sees white-light, while Allen continues to just see purple and/or green-light and the Reiki-sensations.

In summation, vivid colors, lights, symbols, tingling in their hands and nose, all of this and more have been experienced by the students of either the Mystical or Chakral Meditations. In their earnest efforts to evolve, my various meditation students who faithfully continue to attend these regular, weekly gatherings, are still experiencing these glimpses, which are both fascinating and encouraging to them. Many still insist that they are seeing their "angels" and "spirit-guides", past-lives, etc.

The conclusions I have come to thus far, based on the total almost a year's worth of observation and questioning of the attendees of the regular Mystical and Chakral-Meditation are this: generally, they seem to be intellectually and emotionally satisfied with these experiences.

The Wednesday-night, or Mystical Meditation nights yield spiritual/ God-oriented results/experiences, and have helped to improve the quality of the attendees lives via their improved self-esteem. The oneness with God that occurs, whether they are consciously aware or not, at the very least, benefits them spiritually.

The Thursday-night, or Chakral Meditation nights afford more paranormal/psychic experiences. These have generally resulted in an "entertainment value" for the attendees, as they continue to faithfully attend weekly for these experiences. All believe that their psychic-abilities have improved as a result of participating on the Thursdays, many of them describing specific experiences.

Again, I am thankful that they are also having Divine-contact/union, allowing them all of the aforementioned benefits of this.

The Findings

As just described, my meditation-students' experiences are wide and varied, but I can sum them up thusly: 99% believe they are making contact/union with God. The reasons for this are mainly because of the conscious experiences they are having, for example, the green or purple lights they are seeing. 30 % of this 99% who believe they are achieving Divine-contact are having these purple or green-light experiences. Of this 99% as well, the other 30% are seeing an "eye", white-light, a "brushing up against them" of something. This 60% of conscious experiences are convincing the 99-percentile that they are making Divine contact. Those believing they are consciously making Divine-contact feel relieved, protected, excited/enthusiastic.

One can sub-divide this 99-percentile into those who believe they are having some sort of paranormal experience, into the various paranormal experiences that they are apparently experiencing. Approximately 20% are seeing what they believe are their angels, guides, and/or animal-guides. They clearly describe the sex, hair-color, manner of dress, and style/color(s) of wings, if any! They describe what manner of beast (lions, bears, black panther, etc.) they have "seen" around them as well. They describe a feeling of excitement and satisfaction at this. Another 10% believe they are seeing their own Past-Lives, and describe the environment, manner of dress of others, even who they believe these people are in relation to their current-lifetime! This provides amazement, enthusiasm and relief that they apparently have an understanding of who they are now, and why others have reincarnated again into this lifetime. Less than 10% believe that they are "seeing" during meditation either into alternate dimensions/astral-worlds of the dead (where they describe clearly a dearly-departed, who gives them reassurance), or a past-life on "Atlantis" where they describe vivid images of molten-like, or fluid-like multi-colored fields, mountains, and red-skies! They will often describe the architecture as resembling early/ancient Greece/Rome. The people they encounter often resemble those they know in this lifetime, however dressed in ancient Grecian/Roman garb. Often, they will "ride" on a "dolphin" through air and sea! This makes them feel amazed and bewildered. They wish to draw and/or paint these images. Within this less than 20% are those who believe they have travelled, during meditation, to alternate "worlds"/dimensions, perhaps of an "extraterrestrial"-realm. They describe non-threatening "alien-beings" which makes them feel both curious and uncomfortable. It is the appearance of these aliens (either large, insect-like creatures, or the often-described diminutive, grey-skinned, large-eyes/head creatures) which makes them feel uncomfortable. They also vividly describe exotic vegetation and flora which apparently exist on these worlds.

Regardless of this subdivision of paranormal experiences, those involved completely feel safe "in God's hands" and/or believe that God is giving them these experiences for reasons as of yet unknown to them. Regardless, they feel positive overall.

Upon further questioning of the attendees to both the Mystical and Chakral Meditations, all feel relaxed and happy. Ten-percent feel that they are "on-track" with their "soul's purpose" or why they are really here, incarnated into this life. They believe that they are here to help others to heal themselves. It is encouraging to note that another 40% are passionate about entering into, or having recently entered into, the healing arts/alternative wellness. These 40% had been working at other jobs/careers that they no longer felt passionate about, are are now achieving a modicum of personal, if not professional/financial success.

All attendees feel an overall improved quality of life, since regularly meditating over a year, noticing that there is more of a "flow"/synchronicity. They all, too, feel more relaxed overall, and speak of responding to situations, rather than reacting. Most are speaking of increased self-esteem and confidence, more readily going for that new job, relationship, situation, etc. when previous to regularly meditating, they would have hesitated or not pursued these things at all.

I must note here, that from a therapeutic or clinical perspective, my hypnotherapy patients have been making quicker progress in the areas of improved self-esteem, and/or weight-loss. That's not to say that the meditation students are not making progress in these areas, merely slower. It is my theory that because my hypnotherapy patients come to me with a focused intention of altering some unwanted behavior in their life, within a specific and finite time-frame, that they succeed quicker. With my meditation students, the lessening of unwanted behavioral patterns occurs as a "bonus" or after-effect, if you will, because the students' main goals with meditation are Divine-contact and paranormal experiences, without specific deadlines or time-frames.

Only 2% of my meditation students have lost weight significantly, mainly as a result of relaxing more, and feeling better about themselves, thus altering slightly their lifestyles and diet, naturally and gradually. Many have stopped/slowed-down smoking naturally, again, as a result of feeling better with meditation, as opposed to taking in that smoke. As for things like major addictions to drugs and alcohol, I have not yet personally encountered patients or students under this category.

Finally, based on the findings/results of a year's worth of observation of the Mystical as well as Chakral Meditation students, that the mind/body/soul benefits for these students (that is to say emotional/psychological, financial, spiritual) have far exceeded any expectations I, or they, might have initially had.

Discussion of Findings

What exactly are the implications of these findings? How can these findings affect society as a whole? What are the implications of these findings both from a clinical as well as a spiritual and metaphysical perspective? How might the Metaphysician as well as the Clinical Therapist benefit professionally? Similarly, what are the potential benefits, physically, emotionally, and spiritually for the clients of Metaphysicians and Clinical Therapists long-term? What are the potential benefits, physically, emotionally, and spiritually for the clients of Metaphysicians and Clinical Therapists long-term?

What follows now, will be a discussion of this.

Based on the findings previously outlined of my students of both types of meditations which I facilitated over the past year, it is encouraging to note that regardless of what specific experiences, feelings, etc. the participants were having, that Meditation is definitely a "gateway" to Metaphysics, as is Yoga. (Masters, 1989)

Whether it is "Western" Meditation, (Masters, 1989) whose primary goals are relaxation and/or elimination of unwanted thought-patterns, such as negative self-esteem, or "Eastern Meditation", or "Mystical Meditation", (Masters, 1989) whose primary objective is union with the Divine, all the subjects expressed enthusiasm to go on and regularly attend, due in part, to the experiences they were having, which due to a curiosity factor, created a drive about continuing, and/or because of their desire to be the best they can be._ie-develop spiritually. Regardless of their motives, the mere act of meditating would encourage a therapeutic, healing effect on a mind/body/soul level, whether they were consciously aware of this or not, in addition to evolving spiritually. (Masters, 1989)

The fact that many of them have gone on to study a number of other healing-modalities, such as Crystal and Theta healing, and Lomi Lomi Massage, which they have stated, was as a result of their own positive meditative experiences, their motivation being to help themselves and others, is also encouraging. One of them has even gone on to specialize in using Reiki to help animals to heal, all because of her "increased sensitivity" to apparently knowing what those animals feel, or an increased "empathy", if you prefer.

Allan's apparent increased ability to "see" or "know" more, which he attributes to regular meditation, encouraged him to study the Theta modality, which he is excelling at, he informed us. He claims that he can "see" the non-physical trouble-areas of the clients, due in part, he credits, to meditating regularly: again, an increase in psychic/paranormal abilities and empathy.

Whether it is because these Meditators are becoming more easily one with the Universal-Consciousness, (Seale, 1986) and therefore "knowing" tandemly what the clients are "knowing" unconsciously about what they are really needing, and/or whether they are merely increasing their own sensitivities on one level or another, is not important: they are nonetheless feeling encouraged to evolve spiritually, and to help others.

Because this study only involved people already open to/interested in the study of the paranormal and spirituality, it is difficult to arrive at conclusions to society as a whole, in regards to those who are more of a "clinical" nature. Perhaps as the general public is exposed to movies and television that depict the paranormal and spiritual in a positive light, (as of these writings, there are numerous television programs and movies about mediumship and ghosts) perhaps this will be a gateway, if you will, for the broad public to lean towards exploring these areas, Meditation being one direction; we can only hope that they explore it from this perspective of the "Mystic", (God-centered) rather than the short-term/superficial "Psychic" (paranormal) perspective.

Nonetheless, from the Metaphysician's perspective, it is obvious how the use of Meditation (both Eastern and/or Western) benefits their patients, if they prefer Meditation over Hypnosis: improved self-esteem, exploration/healing of the mind/body/soul, even weight-loss; it is a gateway to more matters spiritual, and thus, increases the patient's odds of evolving/healing on all levels. At the very least, Meditation provides relaxation/stress-management.

From the more clinical Therapist's perspective, Meditation accomplishes all that Hypnotherapy accomplishes, without the conscious aim of healing the mind/body/soul: it still reconditions the mind to function in a less dysfunctional/neurotic manner, by getting to the "root-causes" of the unwanted behaviors, just as Meditative Mind-Treatments heal the traumas in the Personal Subconscious which are the "root-causes" of the limited/limiting thoughts/behavior of the patient. (Seale, 1986)

It is not important whether the Meditators in this study continue on from a Metaphysical perspective, or move towards a more clinical Therapist's perspective, as long as they employ Meditation and/or Hypnosis as part of the treatments of their patients; this way, the clients will be ensured at least of a base of spirit, or God, which is the basis of all true healing. (Masters, 1989)

Results

According to all these findings, it is easy to see how Meditation provides satisfaction for the Metaphysician, as well as potentially, for the more clinical therapist. The sensations, visuals, etc. experienced during Meditation, encourage even the most jaded, clinical person to at least consider the concept/possibility that more exists beyond the known five senses, especially when they know what scientists and medical doctors have proven: that under hypnosis or meditation, the mind cannot make up things!

How can one argue, then, the validity of the experiences of these people, places, lights, symbols, sounds, etc., etc. during Meditation, Western or Eastern? How can one dispute the existence of anything more than the five senses, when the implication, therefore, of these experiences, being real, exist deep within the unconscious mind, where, according to Jung, we have stored symbols, archetypes and concepts of ourselves? (Masters, 1989) In other words, a greater Knowing/Understanding of ourselves exists deep within ourselves, within our unconscious mind. This has already been long-proven. That through the "key" of hypnosis, or meditation, (again, which scientists have proven to be the same brainwave-state) the unconscious human-mind may be opened, and thus, explored. How can anyone argue, therefore, that through this "tapping" if you will, of the human unconscious-mind, be it through Meditation or Hypnosis, that any and all dysfunctions, problems, and traumas exist, and may be uncovered and healed?

This is not a new concept: sages throughout time have spoken of this; in modern times, Freud, Jung, Quimby, have all spoken of and/or proven that through opening/contact with the unconscious human-mind, limitless potential exists.

Whether it is through the techniques of Self-Hypnosis/Hypnosis or Meditation which make direct contact with the unconscious levels of the human-mind, it does not matter. A greater understanding of one's Self occurs; even a healing, mind, body, and soul, occurs. Whether the patient describes past-lives they are seeing; whether they recall a trauma from this life or a previous one; whether they are enjoying a journey of the mind, and are seeing exotic places, meeting familiar or new people, animals, or angels and guides; whether they are taking time to focus in on the energy-centers, or "chakras" within their body; whether they are seeing a light, color or colors. These experiences specific and unique only to them, serve merely as encouragement, an acknowledgement by their unconscious-mind, a signpost if you will, that they are on the right track. Even if the experiences are not always positive, it is still created by God, deep within them, so that they may explore these experiences, and heal themselves with God's unconscious guidance. Sometimes we call this unconscious guidance gained/developed through regular Meditation, "Intuition". A greater development of one's Intuition is another sign of one's spiritual growth through Meditation. Even paranormal/psychic experiences are signs of one's spiritual growth, gained through meditation/self-hypnosis/hypnosis.

It does not matter whether the clinical Therapist formally employs Western or Eastern Meditation or not, as part and parcel of the modalities/services they provide; it is, as already stated, to the benefit of their clients that they at least do provide Hypnosis, Self-Hypnosis, or Hypnotherapy as a form of treatment for uncovering unconscious issues. Hypnosis has certainly become more widely accepted and used in recent times; (Masters, 1989) so has Meditation, even with a minority of clinical Therapists, who now often recommend it to their patients as a form of stress-management, as do many corporations encourage it on their employees breaks; and certainly with most Metaphysicians, as part of their practice.

The broad, general public has embraced Meditation more and more in recent times as well, since the Maharishi and the Beatles brought it to the attention of the west in the 1960's. (Masters, 1989)

Whether it be the private person, professional or non-professional, the Metaphysician, or clinical Therapist personally or professionally employing it, Meditation/Hypnosis continues to grow in popularity, providing a key to the wonders of the mind and the universe, through the exploration of the Universe within the Mind.

CHAPTER 2

▼

The Human Mind: A Metaphysical Therapist's Perspective

The study of Metaphysics, academically in the west as stated earlier, is traditionally grouped under the category of "Speculative Philosophy". In popular western culture, matters "metaphysical" often include subjects pertaining to the paranormal, e.s.p., (or extra sensory perception) ghosts, spirits, astrology, divination, the "New Age" movement, self-help, etc. In the east and far-east, thousand-year-old subject-matter/traditions that in the west are considered "metaphysical" include meditation, study of the "chakras", or energy-centers of the body, "Pranic"-breathing and yoga, to name just a few. These ancient Sanskrit health-maintaining, spiritual practices are grouped under the category of "mysticism" and "metaphysics" in the west.

Thanks to modern-day western authors, therapists and psychologists such as Carl Jung, ("Collective Unconscious" theories and "Transpersonal Psychology") Phineas Parkhurst Quimby, (father of the "New Thought" movement) Ernest Holmes, (author of "Science of Mind" and "Religious Science" and "Unity" movements) Milton Erickson, (creator of N.L.P.) and

Aaron T. Beck, ("Cognitive Behavior" creator) to name but a few, we have a melding of eastern "metaphysics" and western psychology, which we shall call "Spiritual" or "Metaphysical Psychology".

Metaphysical Psychology and Western Psychology

Very basically, western psychologists define a "neurotic" mind as one that cannot relate to, or adapt to, its exterior environment. When this occurs, the therapist trains and treats the mind to relate to whatever current, exterior environmental situation exits, so that the person being treated does not retreat into a fantasy-world situation created by their mind. Unfortunately for the patient, their environment will inevitably change, evolve, and grow again, upon which time further analysis/psychological treatment will be required again for their adapting to these new changes. Western psychology therefore fails as far as permanent results for the patient are concerned.

Eastern, or "Spiritual/Metaphysical Psychology" provides a permanent solution for the patient, whereby no ongoing, or occasional "upgrading" is required.

How is this accomplished?

We must delve a little deeper into the nature of western and Metaphysical Psychology to understand this.

Western psychology provides as an "anchor" or basis of the human-mind the "Libido", or "Survivor-Instinct" which apparently (according to western psychology) exists in the "Personal Subconscious"-level of the mind, just beneath the "Conscious"-level of the mind. Within this "Personal Subconscious" mind also exists memories accumulated from events that occurred in the "Conscious" awareness/physical environment of the subject. Both western and Metaphysical Psychologists agree on the existence of the "Conscious" and "Personal Subconscious" (or "Memory-Bank") levels of the mind. Metaphysical, or Spiritual Psychology deviates from western psychology after that.

Metaphysical Psychologists believe that the basis or "anchor" of the human-mind is not the Libido, but God, Perfect-Mind, or Source. Furthermore, several other levels of the mind exist, according to Spiritual/Metaphysical Psychology. One level up from the center, or God, or "Perfect Mind" exists what Carl Jung called the "Collective Unconscious", wherein we hold "archetypes" or symbolic-representations of people we have encountered in our environment, or Conscious-level of our mind. Jung referred to these archetypes as the "gods and goddesses" of our mind. More accurately, someone who may have hurt us in the past may be represented unconsciously as a "demon" or "devil", or a "temptress", "shrew", "whore", etc. The patient may therefore see themselves symbolically and unconsciously at that level of their mind as a "victim". Conversely a healthy mind may contain images of the owner of the mind as the "artist", "seeker", "prince", "princess", "Mother Goddess", etc. In theory, from a metaphysical perspective, these unconscious archetypes (or how the patient unconsciously "sees" themselves and others) will cause them to give out a certain "vibe", which will often translate/extend to the physical. How often have we seen people shuffling along, head lowered and shoulders drooped, with very little energy? Often these people are not even consciously aware of their feelings/emotions/visuals of themselves! We might say that "life" has caused them to be "worn down". In extreme cases, this vibration/resonation/unconscious attitude begins to affect the physical health of the person, let alone their emotional well-being. This level of the mind that holds the vibration of the person's archetypes is called the "Psychic-Energy Level", because the person will give out on a "psychic (or non-physical) energy-level a "feeling" or resonation or vibration of how they really see themselves and others unconsciously. This is often why a person who is resonating out anger or bitterness will attract to themselves someone with a similar vibration: either attracting conflict, or friends/partners or "birds of a feather" who "flock together". "Misery loves company". Happiness/positive attitude attracts and perpetuates happier people and situations.

Similarly, when there are two pianos in a room, and a note is struck in one piano, the same string will resonate by itself, and automatically, within the other piano. Try this.

The next levels up from the center is the Personal Subconscious or Memory-Bank, and Conscious-level as previously discussed.

The Metaphysical Psychologist therefore has a chance to work with more levels of a person's mind to help them more completely and permanently resolve the patient's emotional hindrances, with God as the basis, as opposed to the ever-changing physical environment as a basis.

Psycho-Physical Unit

In Metaphysical Science and Psychology, the term "Psycho-Physical Unit" refers to the fact that the mind affects the body (as previously discussed) and the body affects the mind, for example, if you are not feeling physically well, you often are not feeling happy or in a good mood. Which came first? The bad mood which caused the physical issue, or vice-versa? This is also another basis of a branch of metaphysics called "New Thought", recently brought to mass consciousness by the DVD "The Secret", but originally observed, documented, and practiced in mid-1800's eastern United States by Phineas Parkhusrt Quimby. (Seale, 1986)

Quimby was a clockmaker, who used hypnosis (then called "Mesmerism" named after the 18th-century German therapist and practitioner Franz Anton Mesmer) to cure his patients of physical and emotional illnesses. He did this by "magnetizing" them. The word "magnetizing" at the time was interchangeable with hypnotizing/putting into trance/meditative-state of the client or patient. Quimby would then use suggestions similar to what Milton Erickson would later develop as N.L.P. or Neuro-Linguistic Programming, to change the negative thinking of the patient, substituting positive for negative thought-patterns. This was also the forerunner to Clinical Hypnotherapy. If appropriate for the particular patient, (who at the time was often religious) Quimby would quote religious scripture while they were hypnotized/in meditative-state to "prove" and "talk the patient out of" negative thinking. This was the forerunner to Ernest Holmes' Religious Science/Science of Mind and Unity. One of Quimby's many successes was a patient whose name was Mary Baker Eddy. Her husband, a medical doctor, took his invalid wife to see Quimby. She was bedridden for many years, but after Quimby cured her, she could walk, spreading and practicing this new therapy/movement that she called New Thought for many years after Quimby's death.

To say that Quimby "cured" his patients would be inaccurate, and Quimby himself would no doubt agree: the patients cured themselves. His use of meditation/mesmerism/hypnosis so that the patients "new thoughts" would impact more greatly on their unconscious mind and therefore affect in positive ways their emotional and physical health is a more accurate description.

One might therefore, in Metaphysical terms, say "the spirit (God) heals the soul, which heals the mind, which heals the body". Quimby used whatever verbage he was guided to use, to convince/argue/explain to the heart and soul of the patient (their mind) of the cause of their illness, helping them see the illogic of it (again, in their mind), which in turn helped them emotionally to feel better immediately with this "knowing", and consequently eliminate the physical symptoms. He said "the reason for the illness is the cure".

In metaphysics it is believed that the mere practice of meditation heals the person, because this practice of "Divine Union"/Mystical Meditation/ Divine Contact whether conscious or not, heals the soul which heals the mind which heals the body. We are Psycho-Physical units.

All of this came about because of Quimby's studies, documentation, and practice. Today we recognize in western psychology that meditation/hypnosis makes the mind more susceptible to suggestions, therefore if the therapist logically reasons out the source of the patient's issues, the information will sink deeper into their mind, and be more long-lasting. If the therapist (as in Metaphysical Psychology) heals/changes the patients archetypes within the

Collective Unconscious, as well as the traumas within the memory-bank, or Personal Subconscious of their mind, at the same time, under hypnosis/ meditation creating a safe and permanent Higher Authority/situation (God, or the patient's concepts of God, again, permanently fixed in their unconscious mind, and substituted for anything negative via hypnosis/meditation), then this is in Metaphysical Psychology referred-to as a Meditational, or Metaphysical/Spiritual Mind-Treatment. Many of the techniques found in western psychology, therefore, have their roots in eastern/spiritual mysticism, including the use of hypnosis, or meditation.

One may see now how the aforementioned western psychological modalities such as N.L.P., Clinical Hypnotherapy, and even Cognitive Therapy (which seeks to help the client overcome difficulties by identifying and changing dysfunctional thinking, behavior, and emotional responses. This involves helping clients developing skills for modifying beliefs, identifying distorted thinking, relating to others in different ways, and changing behaviors) were influenced by these earlier Metaphysicians such as Quimby, Holmes, and even Jung.

Part 2-

God: Religion, Theology, Philosophy, Spirituality, and Metaphysics

▼

Definitions and Semantics

For the purposes of this text, and from a therapist's perspective, "God" will be the "glue", if you will that not only "binds" everything together, but that which heals and cures everything. It is the "anchor", or thing that we substitute in the patient's mind, for the debilitating traumas, thoughts, incidents, etc. It doesn't matter what their theological leanings are, or even their philosophical, or psychological leanings. As long as they believe in a concept of "God" or something greater than themselves that they can relate to; all the better if they philosophize and theorize about God's existence; even the theoretical stumbling-block of the potential patient being atheistic or agnostic, does not interfere with this process. Thus far, as I've said before, I have not yet had an Agnostic or Atheist come to me for guidance, again, likely because of the "spiritual"-nature of Metaphysics.

As stated earlier, it is because of the very structure/belief-system of these "metaphysical/spiritually-based philosophies" that I teach and practice, if embraced by the clients or patients, that actually binds the person's mind to become one with itself, or becomes healed. It is because the very nature of these metaphysical philosophies, which satisfy the querant's mind, soon turning everything into a "science", rather than a "philosophy". Perhaps it is because of the many early years of research and proof/results "in the field" of those who have come before me, that turns it all from theory and philosophy, to proven "science". I will often quote P.P. Quimby's works as a means of "legitimizing" in the eyes of my clients, these techniques; Quimby, and his hundreds of documented successes with his patients, along with his years of documented proven theories, (after all, is not science merely proven theories?) leaves little, if anything, to the imagination, or to doubt or question. All that is considered New Thought/Metaphysics has been proven in years of ongoing documented practice and results. I am proud to say that the same has been occurring for myself and my patients and clients.

From Theory to Reality

During the intake, (or early, information-gathering part of the session) I determine what the patient's views are on "God". I will outwardly ask them, "Do you believe in God?" Their responses will range from a resounding "Yes!" to: "I believe in something greater than me," or even "I like to to say "Light"," or "I use the word "Creator".

The very fact that I am a Doctor of Metaphysical Science attracts to me a clientele that at the very least would like to believe in "God", whether they will admit it or not. The fact that I am also an Ordained Metaphysical Minister even more so attracts a non-secular group of clients and patients. "Traditional" therapists, counselors, psychologists, and psychiatrists by the very nature of their title will draw to them both secular and non-secular clientele, rarely exclusively secular, and yet, rarely exclusively non-secular.

I will often make it appear as if I use the word "God" purely for semantics; that indeed, we can easily substitute the word "God" for "Creator", "Higher Power", "Universal Mind", "Source", etc. This methodology/handling early on of the patient has thus far always resulted in me not alienating myself from them. Perhaps they see my enthusiasm; perhaps they share my excitement; regardless, I establish early on that we are on the same "wavelength", and that we are proceeding smoothly. This is how I have always been able to work with all sorts of clients, regardless of their theological and philosophical backgrounds.

Ironically, it has been a minority of members of extreme religious groups that I have had to turn away, for they either believe that meditation, and/or certainly hypnosis is the "work of the devil", or because I am not quoting scripture profusely enough for them! They seem to "slip through the cracks" so that they can see me face-to-face and rant on. These fanatics generally are less-educated and/or are sometimes not psychologically well, but initially manage to fool me into me granting them a partial session, at least. I respectfully usher them out, encouraging them to read their relevant scripture of choice, and saying "God bless you." This is why the initial phone-call of inquiry is so crucial for screening out potential "time-wasters" (and I mean time-wasters for the both of you). Establishing early on in their phone inquiry if they were referred to you (my preference) from an existing client, along with what they hope to accomplish in the session, is crucial for avoiding wasting everyone's time. If I realize that one of my peers can be of greater service to the phone-inquirer, then I certainly recommend them to see that person.

It is during the intake, when the potential (and screened) client is sitting before me, that I must help to encourage any beliefs/theories of "God" that they may have, and transform them into reality in their eyes and minds, as it were.

"God" is the "magic wand", the "maker of miracles", the stuff healing and transformation is made of. At least, the client must believe this.

This is reinforced by associating "the power of their mind" with "God".

I always explain during the intake about the scientifically-proven documentation of the two halves of the human brain: one half being the logical, reasoning, thinking part, and the other half being the creative, or "God-Mind" part. The logical part of the brain will always make us worry more, thinking, perhaps, too much about our problems in an attempt to find a logical solution. The God-Mind part of the brain is always pure faith: a deep-down knowing that things always work out for the best. It is this healing, all-powerful "God-Mind" part of the brain that we will be concentrating on during the session, I emphasize to the patient at this point

The Power of the Mind and Muscle-Testing

I then accomplish the patient's melding/associating the healing, transformative power of their mind/brain as being their "God-Mind" in a number of ways. Firstly, I show them color diagrams of the mind as it is depicted in western/traditional psychology, and then I show them the multi-layered mind within the system of eastern/holistic/metaphysical psychological beliefs. I show how the origins of these eastern beliefs are rooted in many thousands of years of proof and practice. I then briefly compare the limiting beliefs of western psychology to limitless eastern healing techniques and practices of the mind, showing how western therapy is lengthy and temporary, since the "anchor" is the patient's physical, exterior environment at the time of therapy, versus the anchor in eastern therapy being the eternal, or God part of the mind. They begin to understand early how the outside is always changing, but the interior, God-at-the-centre-of-the-mind is consistent and eternal. The diagrams seem to provide a "clinical/scientific" feel to the information I am giving, thus legitimizing it.

With this "theory" of the power of the mind out of the way, we then concentrate on the "reality" of the power of the mind.

I remind them how during crises, many times it has been reported that a physically small/weak person will lift a car, or exhibit "super-human" strength in order to save their child or loved one. This is the conscious, "human-mind" being by-passed by the greater unconscious "God-Mind" to accomplish the "un-accomplishable"! This example always rings true for them. It is a thumbnail encapsulation of the virtually untapped "Power of the Mind", or "Pure God-Mind" in action. This seems to also meld/connect the "power of the Mind" with the strength of "God"/"God-Mind".

Next, we do "muscle-testing", which is based on Kineseology, also known as "Human Kinetics", or the science of how the human body moves.

This "testing" is based on the proven theory that the human subconscious-mind unconsciously affects the functioning of the physical body. We sit on straight-backed chairs, face-to-face, knees touching, with a pillow laying flat on our knees, as a sort of "working-surface"…really, it is to put the subject at ease during the treatment. I then ask the subject to make an "o" with the second-finger and thumb of their dominant-hand, pressing as tightly together as they possibly can, to resist the counterforce of the same dominant fingers of my hand; in other words, we are connected via the two "o's" we have both made with the two fingers of our dominant-hands. I explain that when one lies, no matter how convincingly, there is still a physiological response: either sweating, eyes darting back and forth, pulse racing, blood-pressure rising, etc; it is why/how lie-detectors work. I declare to my patient that we will now do a sort of "human lie-detector" test, and when he/she says a falsehood, as it is human-nature, they will become weaker than they normally would be, but when they are telling the truth, they will maintain their physical strength, and be able to resist my pulling free from their "o". Of course, this always works: I get them to say their name, their sex, their age, and I cannot break free of the thumb/finger-loop/"o"; then I ask them to say a specified lie, and sure enough, I pull my "o" free from theirs, each time they tell a lie.

This proves to them that there is something greater than themselves: their "God-Mind" /the power of the mind, and its effects on the human-body. Later, after the Mind-Treatment is completed, we do the muscle-testing again, and when I get them to say a positive-reinforcement statement/belief relevant to their treatment, such as "I love myself" or "I am healed", etc. etc., their strength remains and they cannot break the finger-loop; conversely when they tell a lie again, the loop is broken! This reinforces/proves to them that the therapy worked, and that they are healed. They always, at this point, believe that the power of the mind that healed them was also God's power, or the "God-Mind" part of their brain/mind.

Eye-To-Eye

We always sit as per the previous description with the pillow, to establish a sort of intimacy/opening up/letting go, without the vulnerability; the pillow acts as a sort of "buffer". Also, psychologically it is a "safe place" for the patient's hands to conveniently drop to during the session, and for me to be able to more easily access their hands for re-assurance during the treatment, without me taking my eyes off of their eyes.

The "eye-to-eye" technique originated in the inaccurate assumption in the early years of "mesmerism" or hypnosis in the 1700's that the "mesmerizer" exuded some sort of "power" over the subject via the eyes. In reality, the subject must continually focus on a focal-point, whether it be the auditory droning on and suggestions of the practitioner, the monotonous ticking of a clock/pendulum, or the subject staring, eyes closed, inward and upward at their third-eye/brow-region; physiologically, this creates a calming effect, similar to when the subject stares upward and back at a spot on the ceiling, a swinging pocket-watch, or light. The combination of the staring/straining of the eyes slightly upward and back causes the eyes to gently close, while the verbal suggestions of the practitioner go deeper into the patient's subconscious because they are more "open" to suggestions during this light-trance/daydream-like state, also called "Alpha"; the suggestions will go deeper and even more permanently into the subject's subconscious if they drift a little deeper into near-sleep state, or "Theta" brainwave state.

It has been my experience as both a Clinical Hypnotherapist and teacher of Meditation for many years that it isn't imperative that the subject keeps their eyes closed: they will no more or less be "under" either way! The therapy is neither more nor less effective with eyes opened or closed: for example, notice how often we are standing at a line-up at the checkout of a grocery-store, we stare off into Alpha, or daydream-state so naturally, with our eyes opened; or when we are driving for a long time, then suddenly forget where we are going, or have missed our turn-off: again; we "drifted off", with our eyes opened!

From a psychological perspective, the sessions seem more intense to my patients when their eyes have remained opened, fixated on my own, as compared to sessions I have done with their eyes closed; the experiences seem more real to them, when they have had their eyes open, than with their eyes closed; I believe they think they have dreamt it all when they have had their eyes closed, or even that they have made things up. It has already been clinically proven that a subject cannot make things up during hypnotic/meditative-state: the creative part of their brain becomes inactive in that state.

Later on, I will go into detail and describe specifically step-by-step, the techniques of these "miracle" Mind Treatments.

CHAPTER 2

▼

Myths Exploded: Hypnosis and Meditation, the Keys to the Mind

Hypnosis and Meditation as Practical Tools

I find it necessary to explore Hypnosis vs. Meditation at this point primarily because I have seen incredible breakthroughs for my clients and patients as a result of all of these practices, and the similarities between the two methods/ modalities. In fact, for the purposes of this book, you may interchange/ substitute one word for the other, if you wish.

It has been my professional observation over the years, that, "Clinical" Hypnotherapists will often limit their practice to employing Hypnosis only, while often ignoring and neglecting Meditation, even when qualified and capable of practicing it, for their clients, if that method might better suit the "personality" or receptiveness of that client.

I intend to clearly define now the terms "Clinical Hypnotherapy", "Meditation", and "Self-Hypnosis", and I also intend at this point to describe the techniques, goals and brainwave-states unique and common to

Hypnosis and Meditation, and the specific, unique and common benefits that Meditation and Hypnosis has had on my patients.

In addition, I will shortly illustrate how Clinical Hypnotherapists may apply Meditation or Self-Hypnosis for the Metaphysical as well as non-Metaphysical (Clinical) benefit of their patients, as well as how Practitioners of Metaphysics/Meditation Teachers may apply "Clinical" Hypnosis for the Metaphysical and non-Metaphysical (Clinical) benefit of their students and clients. I intend to do this by again sharing a number of practical examples from my case-files. Of course, the names and details of my clients have been changed to maintain their anonymity.

It is my hope, that by writing this chapter, that more Metaphysicians and Clinical Hypnotherapists will also successfully treat and assist their clients, students, and patients in re-empowering themselves, by not limiting themselves or their clients, to employing one method over the other.

You decide: "Hypnosis or Meditation as practical tools?"

The Study

Most of the potential clients who approached me about Hypnotherapy as a means of altering unwanted behavior such as smoking, fear elimination, low self-esteem, and over-eating, generally, I have discovered, did not concern themselves with, nor did they necessarily believe in living a spiritual existence, nor did they particularly have an interest in, or belief in

Metaphysics, or Meditation. There was even a certain amount of skepticism on their part about the effectiveness of Hypnosis!

This is ironic, as daydream, Meditative, light-Hypnotic and "Alpha" brainwave-states have been scientifically measured and proven to be identical, according to Shields (1986).

These potential clients were, however, generally on a journey of self-improvement and growth.

Those who inquired about Hypnotherapy as a means of exploring past and

between-life existences, discovering their angels and guides, etc., had a definite interest in things Metaphysical, we had observed. They, despite, belief in the effectiveness of

Hypnosis, had sometimes requested Guided-Visualizations, and/or Meditations to accomplish all of this, instead of Hypnosis, because they did not realize that it is all the same thing, that is to say, the brainwave-state under light-Hypnosis, is the same as a Meditative, and/or daydream-state, according to Shields. (1986)

They sometimes doubted that they could be hypnotized, in which case I provided for them the statistics that only two- percent of the population cannot be hypnotized, as stated by Shields (1986). I then went on to explain and to define, in scientific terms, the hypnotic-state, comparing it to a daydream-like state, as stated by Hewitt (2004).

We did suggestibility tests, as described by Hathaway (2003) or susceptibility test, as referred-to by Shields (1986), with these potential clients, which proved to both the potential patient and the Practitioner that they (the potential patient) could indeed be hypnotized.

They too, were on a journey of self-discovery and growth.

Those who had approached me to teach them Meditation, were more concerned with matters Metaphysical, as opposed to the logistical, problem-solving, areas of life, we learned. They generally, intended to use Meditation as a means of stress-alleviation and/or experiencing God.

Often unaware of the other, practical benefits of Meditation such as improving self-esteem, stop-smoking, weight-control, lowering blood-pressure, etc., I attempted, occasionally succeeding, in educating them to these facts.

They too, were on a journey of self-discovery and growth.

It is interesting to note that although I had found in my private practice, both group settings and one-on-one, that, for the most part, all of the aforementioned, in regards to clients' requests and needs were generally true, there were some exceptions, although they were few and far between. I am grateful that my professional, as well as my educational background allowed, and still allows me, to provide the choices of either Meditation or Hypnosis for the potential client.

In regards to other professionals and/or Practitioners in the field of Metaphysics, teachers of Meditation and Clinical Hypnotherapists, I hope that there are exceptions to every rule, although, thus far I have yet to discover this.

I can only, therefore, refer to my own professional experiences in regards to employing Meditation in place of Hypnosis, and vice-versa.

That is, sometimes I (as a Clinical Hypnotherapist) will utilize Meditation/Guided Visualizations with a client to alter and improve their self-esteem, or even uncover several previous lives, for the purpose of the client understanding their true nature and purpose this time around. Hopefully other "professional"

Clinical Hypnotherapists will also have the skill and leeway to accomplish this, if he/she is flexible enough to go with the wishes and belief-system of the client.

Someone with little, or no Higher Education/degree, should not attempt any serious therapy with a client for legal and moral reasons. The skills necessary might not be present. This is why, I have found previous to my Clinical Hypnotherapy degree, for example, that practicing/teaching Meditation mainly for the purposes of relaxation, and/or contact with inner Higher Consciousness was acceptable and effective for everyone, as opposed to using Meditation as a means of "problem-solving", that is, altering unwanted behaviors and habits, for example, which is best left to a professional. It is even recommended, that to avoid potentially negative legal ramifications, that rather than, as a Metaphysician, one hypnotizes a client, or engages in "Hetero-Hypnosis," as Masters (1989) refers to it as, that they teach the client how to hypnotize themselves!

I will now discuss some specific cases and instances, where Meditation, Self-Hypnosis, and Hetero-Hypnosis were interchangeable for the particular needs of the client.

From My Case-Book

"Angela" (not her real name) was an attractive, educated, and motivated forty-year-old, with self-esteem issues due to her weight. She was working on losing twenty pounds, and quickly succeeding, when she approached me for Hypnosis for weight-loss. Although she had already been seeing a Hypnotherapist for weight-loss, she was not getting the results she desired. She was somewhat skeptical as to the effectiveness of Hypnosis to begin with, and this was hindering her progress. I suggested that instead of Hypnosis, we could try Meditation as a means of allowing her to "let go" of past, hurtful events, and healing them through "Mind-Treatments Affirmations", as described by Masters. (1989) Furthermore, I suggested, that throughout the weekly Meditation-course that I was offering her, we would also do weekly "Meditational Programming Treatments", as described by Masters, (1989) if she would follow up with her own daily "Mental Rebirth Treatments", as provided by Masters (1989), that I would be teaching her. This, I suggested, would help her to rebuild her self-esteem while she was losing weight, so that she would never again eat to make herself feel good, but merely go inward for strength. In the process, the goal would also be to experience the Divine within. I mentioned that I would teach her a different Meditation technique each week, so that she could decide what worked best for her. She agreed. The first week, we started with the "Candle Concentration Technique" as described by Masters (1973), to get her used to focusing.

One might say that we were doing a kind of Hypnotherapy/Self-Hypnosis program for self-esteem, and indeed, if we did say that, she psychologically wouldn't be open to it, because of the previous ineffectual Hypnosis experiences. The addition of going inward to experience God-Mind/Higher Consciousness/The Divine, etc. made the sessions both Western and Eastern Meditation, according to Masters (1989), as opposed to "Hetero-Hypnosis", as referred-to by Masters (1989) which would have necessitated the use of "Inductions" and "Deepenings" according to Shields (1986) to guide her into an Hypnotic-state, which she didn't want, regardless.

As weeks went on, Angela felt better and better about herself, lost another ten pounds, and could now see light inside of herself with her eyes open or shut, reinforcing her faith/belief in matters Metaphysical! Upon completion of our weekly one-on-one Meditation course, Angela decided to join our weekly group-meditation evenings, which to this day she still attends.

Angela's case clearly shows how Meditation was substituted for Self-Hypnosis, to effectively help her to improve her self-esteem, and eventually to help her to succeed in losing weight.

Further on, you will see an example of Jeff's case, where Self-Hypnosis produced similar results, that of building positive self-esteem.

"Sally", (not her real name) one of my Reiki-students, approached me one day for Hetero-Hypnosis, as referred-to by Masters (1989) to help her release a past emotional trauma, which, she believed, prevented her from attracting and maintaining intimate relationships. Sally was a smart, ambitious, thirty-eight year-old, with a quick, and skeptical mind. The very fact that previously, she requested that I teach her Reiki, a Metaphysically-based system of energy-healing, was a breakthrough for her and her somewhat cynical and skeptical mind. She practiced Reiki regularly on others and herself, for minor issues. This day, she wanted to rid herself of an emotional obstacle that she believed was preventing her from living life to the fullest. She was also consciously aware of what the event was, which made it easier for me. I might have had to employ Hypnosis to also uncover this incident, which could have been locked deep within her unconscious mind, but not in this case. A lot of time and money would now be spared for her.

Because she was aware of the relatively-minor event, I felt that this allowed her the luxury of choosing whether she preferred "Hypnosis or Meditation." She suggested Meditation, not because she was skeptical of Hypnosis, (indeed, her sister was successfully treated previously using Hypnotherapy) but because it felt "less rigid" for her. I agreed.

Because this was "Meditation" and not "Hetero-Hypnosis", or one-on-one Hypnosis, as referred-to by Masters (1989), I didn't have to do a susceptibility test, as described by Shields (1986).

She was already susceptible, willing and comfortable to my guiding her into an altered-state. The fact that she trusted me also helped.

I could proceed, feeling unhindered by an Hypnotic-script, using only improvised guided-visualizations and getting her to focus on her breathing to accomplish what an Hypnotic Induction and Deepening, as described by Shields (1986), would do, which is guiding the patient gently into an altered-state of consciousness, or Meditation, which is the same brainwave-state as being in an Hypnotic-trance, or Alpha brainwave-state, according to Shields (1986). Others, like Hewitt (1997), also refer to this as a "daydream"-state. She had a positive emotional release, as opposed to a negative one, or "abreaction", as described by Shields (1986), which might have occurred had she remembered the actual event, "re-living it," and then letting it go; this is often as traumatic as the original incident.

I have researched that in the long-term, this "re-living" and "letting go" does not benefit the patient, as the unwanted-symptoms caused by the original trauma, often return days, weeks, months, or years later. So why re-traumatize the patient in the first place?

Sally slowly began to welcome into her life intimate relationships, which she has managed,to this day, to maintain, when previously, for her, this was either difficult or impossible.

Sally's case was a successful example of employing Meditation instead of Self-Hypnosis or even Hetero-Hypnosis, as described by Masters (1989), for the purposes of the client re-empowering themselves by releasing a previous trauma. Similar results could have been achieved through Self-Hypnosis. Upon guiding the client into a Self-Hypnotic-trance, utilizing "Inductions" according to Hewitt (1997), "uncovering" methods such as the "Diagnostic-Scanning Technique", referred-to by Shields (1986), or "Free-Floating Regression", as taught by Shields (1986), for determining at what age, and specifically what trauma(s) occurred, and then eventually, employing Self-Hypnosis to "re-program" the person's thoughts and unwanted responses to the past trauma, as per Hathaway (2003).

Teaching Self-Hypnosis to Jeff, a Computer-Technician, was more effective than employing Meditation, in his case, for building and maintaining, positive self-esteem.

Jeff came to me one day, at the suggestion of his friend, a former client of mine. It was my "Clinical Hypnotherapist" degree that made this particular method of self-help more palatable for Jeff, who "avoided New-Age stuff like the plague!" Jeff shared with me, on this particular day, the fact that at thirty-three, he avoided the singles' scene because he was too shy. As a youngster growing up, he was teased by his peers for being over-weight. He had somehow managed to conquer his weight-problem, but not his self-esteem issues. He dated occasionally, but expressed a willingness to date more frequently, and eventually get married, except that he didn't always have the "courage" to ask women out. Other than that, Jeff appeared to be a relatively well-adjusted, well-dressed, affluent, and educated adult.

Self-Hypnosis for building self-esteem was one of my specialties; I even was marketing, at the time, an audio-CD for this purpose. Even if I would have been familiar with, at that moment, the benefits of teaching Meditation for daily Spiritual Mind-Treatments and Spiritual Mental Re-Birth Treatments, as described by Masters (1989), for the purposes of building positive self-esteem, it would still have been appropriate to teach Jeff Self-Hypnosis for building positive self-esteem. He just wasn't comfortable with anything else; he was even familiar with the scientific end of it all, including quoting sources on brainwave-states and their functions.

After determining that Jeff was still a candidate for hypnosis, i.e.- a susceptibility test as taught by Shields (1986), involving his eyes shut tight with arms outstretched, palms up, at my voice suggestions that he imagine a helium-filled balloon was tied to one of his wrists, while in his other palm he held a large, heavy book; one arm went quickly down as the other went quickly skyward, confirming his suggestibility., as described by Hathaway (2003). As well, we determined that he had no contra-indications, as referred-to by Shields (1986), such as depression or anti-depressants taken within the last six-months. I proceeded with a series of long, guided-visualizations, or "Inductions", as well as "Deepenings," as taught by Shields (1986), to insure that Jeff was ready for this six-part therapy. For the Inductions and Deepenings, I decided to use the "sea-shore" and "stairs" visualizations, as taught by Hewitt (1997), initially employing some relaxation-exercises involving visualizing a mountain-top view and meadow, streams, etc. visualization, as described by Goldberg (1998).

I suggested that Jeff will go deeper and deeper each time that he hears my voice, as suggested by Hewitt (1997), to reinforce that listening to the Hypnosis-CD I give my patients at the end of the last treatment, will work. Each time Jeff came for his session, I reinforced a particular positive-self-esteem suggestion, then taught him how he could, anytime, any place, hypnotize himself, giving himself any of the 24 positive self-esteem suggestions from the sheet I supplied him, as well.

Jeff eventually went on to meet, date, and marry the "woman of his dreams", even starting a family.

This was a case where Self-Hypnosis, as opposed to Meditation combined with positive affirmations, was the answer to someone building their self-esteem. I could have easily substituted (had I been familiar with, at the time) Meditation, Spiritual Mind-Treatments, and Positive Affirmations combined with Spiritual Mental Rebirth affirmations/visualizations as taught by Masters (1989), as in Angela's case, for Jeff's growth.

These previous examples from my case-files indicate how Meditation could have easily been substituted for Self-Hypnosis, and vice-versa, for the effective treatment/altering of unwanted behaviors of the particular patient. All that is really needed is the flexibility and education of both the practitioner and the patient.

Findings

Firstly, let's clarify the terms "Hypnosis", "Self-Hypnosis", "Clinical Hypnotherapist" and then "Meditation"

"Hypnosis" and "Self-Hypnosis" are techniques that enable one to achieve an altered-state of Consciousness, (the day-dream state) deliberately, and direct one's attention to specific goals in order to achieve them, as taught by Hewitt (1997). Strictly speaking, the term "Clinical Hypnotherapist" refers to one who has a professional degree in the area of hypnosis and psychotherapy, according to Shields (1986), and may apply this to help patients to rid themselves of unwanted behaviors such as over-eating or smoking, for example, by guiding them into a state of hypnosis using any number of "inductions" or visualizations.

"Self-Hypnosis", according to Shields (1986), may be taught to the patient in order for them to relax more, boost their self-esteem, motivate themselves, and to support their willingness to not smoke, for example. This is accomplished by the patient guiding themselves into an hypnotic-state using their own inductions and visualizations. According to Masters (1989), for legal reasons, the Practitioner should only teach "Self-Hypnosis", rather than practice "Hetero-Hypnosis" i.e., Hypnosis induced upon another. As a Metaphysician and Clinical Hypnotherapist, I have found that employing "Hetero-Hypnosis" for uncovering the previous, and between-life existence of a client rewarding for themselves, as they discover in this way their soul's purpose in this lifetime.

"Meditation", according to Dr. Masters (1989), is accomplished by using one or more methods to withdraw the five senses and the mind from its attention to the world outside oneself and to make contact with the inner mental world of one's own mind. The popularity of Meditation in North America is thanks to the popularity of the Beatles in the 1960's and their teacher, the Maharishi Mahesh Yogi, whom they sought out for personal growth, according to Masters (1989).

Meditation may be divided into "Eastern", or Transcendental (experiencing the God-Mind within) and "Western", or using this altered-state to allow positive prayers and affirmations into one's unconscious mind for the purposes of improving one's "outer-self", referred-to by Masters (1989).

We would also like to clarify, at this point, the individual Hypnotic-states, and their relationship to each other. Scientists, employing a device called an electroencephalogram or EEG, measure and define the various electrical-impulses put out by the human brain during its various stages of consciousness, described by Goldberg (1998). These waves emitted from the brain are measured in "cycles-per-second", or cps. For example, the wide-awake state, or "Conscious Mind Proper", as referred-to by Goldberg (1998), is referred-to as Beta, and is generally 14-20 cps; the "Subconscious Mind", as described by Goldberg (1998), or Alpha-state, is the brainwave-state that most Hypnotherapists desire to get their patients to, for it is the state that allows the patient to be the most open, or susceptible to, positive affirmations and suggestions, in other words, anything said to the patient while they are in Alpha-state will "sink-in" or stay in their subconscious mind. This is the same brainwave-state as "daydream state", and it is also the same brainwave-state as Meditation, although sometimes the Meditative-state will dip deeper, that is, into Theta, as described by Hewitt (1997).

Psychic experiences sometime take place in Alpha, according to Hewitt (1997). It is generally 7-14 cps. Theta's frequency-range is generally 4-7 cps, and this is where hypnosis can sometimes take place as well, suggested Hewitt (1997). All of our emotional experiences seem to be recorded in this state, and is the special range where that opens the door of consciousness beyond hypnosis into the world of psychic phenomena. Theta is the range where psychic experiences are most likely to occur, according to Hewitt (1997). Total unconsciousness is measured at 0 to approximately 4 cps and is called Delta. Not much is known about this range, states Hewitt (1997).

According to Dr. Michael Newton, best known for his "Life-Between-Lives" or "Soul Regression" work, states that there are actually three-levels of Alpha-state: (a) The lighter-stages, used for Meditation, (b) The medium stages, generally associated with recovering childhood traumas, is often useful for behavior modifications such as stop smoking, gaining/losing weight, etc., and (c) The deeper Alpha-states, where past-life recovery is likely to occur, according to Newton (2004). I personally employ Theta-stages for any kind of Past, and/or Soul-Regression work, in addition to stop-smoking and weight-control therapies. I generally employ Meditation (Light-Alpha stages) for behavioral modifications such as building positive self-esteem, which often leads the patient to losing weight on their own. My clients and I have made great strides towards their building their self-esteem through the use of Meditation, as opposed to say, the deeper-stages of Theta, during Self-Hypnosis, which have proven successful for the clients as well. It is often less intimidating for the client, if we use Meditation for the aforementioned purposes, as they may have some issues about being hypnotized, such as skepticism, according to Newton (2004), fear of staying hypnotized, or even of revealing personal secrets, according to Shields (1986).

There are great similarities in the methodologies used in entering into a Meditative, and/or Self-Hypnotic-state.

Firstly, in the initial stages of Hypnosis and Meditation, both attempt relaxation and concentration simultaneously, according to Masters (1989). That is to say, that a focal point of concentration may be utilized, (in Hypnosis, for example, a spiraling hypnotic-wheel, a point on the wall or ceiling, the sound of a metronome; in Meditation, focusing, with closed eyes up into your third-eye, or the use of a candle-flame) in order to achieve a mental-focus and thereby relaxing.

I agree with Dr. Masters (1989) when he states that a Student of Self-Hypnosis is better at practicing Meditation, and a Student of Meditation is better at practicing Self-Hypnosis, because both students are used to the same basic initial methodologies for achieving relaxation and concentration simultaneously. It would, therefore, not be so unimaginable, that if one were to walk down the hallway of an office-building where people were engaging in Meditation in one room and Self-Hypnosis in another room, that one might see a Meditation student sitting, gazing at a candle-flame, and likewise, the student practicing Self-Hypnosis gazing at a bright-light or a pendulum, according to Masters (1989). Both are using a "fixation-object" to concentrate their mind's energies or to achieve mental focus, for the purposes of relaxation.

Insofar as the similar goals of Self-Hypnosis and Western Meditation are concerned, both are essentially concerned with improvement in one's outer self. We have already described how we have helped others to achieve this, employing either Self-Hypnosis or Meditation. Either methodology is as effective.

The only limitations are those imposed by potential patients, or even the Metaphysicians or Clinical Hypnotherapists themselves, often because of the misinformation and lack of acceptance of Hypnosis by the medical profession until recently, and being branded "the work of the devil" by the Christian Science Church, as stated by Masters (1989), and the competence level of the Practitioner themselves, according to Shields (1986).

Recently, I came across a colleague's brochure on Hypnosis, in which I was delighted to find the quote: "All Hypnosis is Self-Hypnosis." This quote, I feel, takes away the potential fear surrounding Hypnosis, legally also shifting the emphasis from "Hetero-Hypnosis", as Masters (1989) calls it, to "Self-Hypnosis", desirable, according to Masters (1989), as previously outlined.

A Clinical Hypnotherapist may insure the reality of this quote thusly: When utilizing susceptibility tests, for example, as taught by Shields (1986), one may determine whether the patient is:

A) Suggestible to direct suggestions from the Hypnotherapist; categorized as "Authoritarian". In my opinion, undesirable, as the goal is always to have the client self-hypnotize themselves.

B) Able to give themselves suggestions internally; categorized as "Permissive". Desirable, because they can tell themselves that it's okay to relax into a Meditative/Self-Hypnotic state, or Alpha using their own will and desire.

C) Able to use their heightened imagination for entering into Self-Hypnosis/Meditation; categorized as "Creative". This is also desirable as they are using their own will/skills to enter into Meditative/Self-Hypnotic state.

The more control of their own free will the client knows they have, and the more the patient participates in the "Induction"-process, the more in control of their free will they will feel they have, and the less fear and resistance they will have entering into Meditative/Self-Hypnotic state.

The client may therefore, truthfully and accurately refer to the process as "Self-Hypnosis" which is more desirable, not "Hetero-Hypnosis", or "Hypnosis". Therefore, the statement "All Hypnosis is Self-Hypnosis" will promote the useful and legal concept/belief that the patient utilizes their own free will to enter into Meditation/Self-Hypnosis. The exception would be with patients who, for whatever reasons, need an authoritarian figure, and/or someone to tell them what to do. They would fall under the susceptibility category of "A", previously referred to above. These patients will willingly and more easily, in my experience, go with the verbal Hypnotherapy inductions/guided-meditations specifically designed to relax them into an altered-state, but strictly speaking, this would be categorized as "Hypnosis"/"Hetero-Hypnosis", not "Self-Hypnosis", in which case a waiver-form, signed by the potential client in any and all cases, could relinquish the Hypnotherapist of any legal and financial responsibilities, in the case of patient dissatisfaction, for whatever their reason.

I have described generally, initial methods for Hypnosis/Meditation common to both, as well as the goals common to both, but let me describe now, in greater detail, the techniques and philosophies that differ between the two, in other words, those that clearly differentiate between Meditation and Self-Hypnosis.

It is crucial that I reiterate, at this stage, what I said earlier about professionals, as opposed to non-professionals, utilizing Hetero-Hypnosis: unless you have some sort of recognized and legal degree/certification/license to practice Hetero-Hypnosis, I recommend against its practice. Employ Meditation. There are no legal requirements, nor are there any therapeutic promises or suggestions in regards to Meditation, other than for promoting relaxation, particularly, in general, with Western Meditation. Utilizing positive affirmations for strengthening self-esteem, in Meditative-state, will accomplish, as I have outlined earlier, just as much as the more lengthy, and costly, Hypnosis for Self-Esteem. If you are blessed enough to have a legal Hypnotherapy degree, then utilization of both, in one's Metaphysical practice, is most desirable, according to Masters (1989).

Strictly speaking, the terms and specific "Inductions" and "Deepenings" techniques, as described by Shields (1986) are exclusively employed in Hypnosis and Hetero-Hypnosis, as opposed to Meditation; but the concentrating inwardly on one's third-eye, and/or mental/verbal uttering over and over of a mantra, or the focusing on one's breathing, as is employed in Meditation, also accomplishes the same goals of focusing and relaxing, but is not referred-to as an "Induction" and "Deepening", when discussing Meditation.

Initially, according to Goldberg (1998), fixation-points such as a candle-flame, or spiraling hypnotic-wheel for relaxation and focusing may be used in Hypnosis, but Inductions and Deepenings as described by Shields (1986) or Hewitt (1997) must eventually be used to guide the subject into a deeper state of Hypnosis. Whereas, with Meditation, the repeated focusing inward, as previously described, results in achievement of the desired Alpha-state, required for both Hypnosis and Meditation. The reasons for the differences are cultural and scientific, that is to say, that Meditation came to North America via the spiritual-mystique of India, (as previously discussed) while Hypnosis and its origins were scientific: During the 1840s and 1850s, according to Hathaway (2003), Dr. Elliotson successfully treated patients for epilepsy, hysteria, headaches and rheumatism using Hypnosis. He also, during this time in England, performed over 200 painless operations, again, employing Hypnosis.

A specific example of an Induction, according to Shields (1986) is a "Progressive Relaxation", where in the subject is asked to concentrate on relaxing each and every part of their body, one-at-a-time. Then, according to Hewitt (1997), a Deepening such as imagining oneself walking down a long and winding staircase, one-step-at-a-time, until one reaches the bottom is employed. A variation of this, according to Shields (1986), is the escalator, or lift (British word for elevator) method, whereby the subject is asked to "see" in their imagination, each numbered-floor lighting up in the elevator, as they are "descending lower and lower, deeper and deeper into relaxation". Of course, one might similarly state here that visualizations are often used in Meditation, which are sometimes referred-to as "Guided Meditations", whereby the Meditator is visualizing themselves walking on a beach, for example, which Hewitt (1997) also employs in Hypnosis.

Again, the end result is common to both Meditation and Hypnosis: entering into the altered-state of Alpha brainwave state.

Discussion of Findings

The findings expressed within this book will impact society in a number of positive ways, provided that these findings are willingly and truly attempted and practiced consistently by professionals in the field of Metaphysics as well as in the field of Clinical Hypnotherapy.

Although the individual levels of competency of these Practitioners will vary greatly due to varying academic and practical experience, in addition to the individualistic views, attitudes and personal perspectives of these Practitioners, in addition to their varying levels of skepticism and confidence, one must still acknowledge the measurable positive impacts of the practices should they be put into general use.

For example, no longer will a patient be limited to the standard choices of treatments, Inductions and Deepenings offered by the Clinical Hypnotherapist, as outlined previously. If the patient feels more comfortable staring at a candle-flame, and focusing on their breath, or sitting cross-legged, mentally repeating an affirmation or mantra for the purposes of entering into an altered level of consciousness, as opposed to staring at a spinning, spiraling Hypnotic wheel, this would now be possible, for that same brainwave-state to be entered into.

Conversely, if the patient feels at home with the more clinical methodology of watching that hypnotic spiraling wheel, versus having incense and New Age music playing in the background as they focus inwardly up into their third-eye, they now have that option for entering into an altered-state of consciousness. If someone wishes to experience their Past Lives, but they feel more comfortable in a more clinical atmosphere, then the Hypnotherapist may guide them into those realms using the more clinical methodologies of hypnotic-wheel, longer Induction and Deepening, etc. Provided that the Metaphysical Practitioner is licensed, and experienced to do counseling, they may effectively use Meditation in place of Hypnosis to aid patients in the areas of self-esteem, weight-control, smoking, current past-life traumas, etc. if the patient feels uncomfortable in a more clinical setting of the Hypnotherapist. That is to say, provided that the academic and legal qualifications of the Metaphysician are met, they may employ their Meditational treatments in place of the Clinical methodologies of the Hypnotherapist, and vice-versa.

This would impact society greatly, as the patient would now have more options and flexibility of choices, in regards to bettering themselves, with lesser personal limitations.

This would also impact society positively, as the professional Metaphysician and Clinical Hypnotherapist could now have greater choices and flexibility of methodologies, in order to assist patients in their betterment.

Both the professional and the patient could potentially grow in experience and flexibility as well. Ultimately, however, what will determine the broader use of these tools, will be the initial flexibility of both patient and Practitioner, as well as the general competency, and recognition of the Practitioner for the need of the use of a methodology not usually employed by them in assisting the specific individual needs, and catering to, the individual belief-system of their patient. Perhaps now, this essay will shed light on these possibilities, and societal benefits.

Summary

It should be clear now, as to what Meditation, Clinical Hypnotherapy, Hetero-Hypnosis and Self-Hypnosis are, the brainwave-state they have in common, as well as the techniques for entering into Self-Hypnosis and Meditative-state, common to each other, as well as differing from each other.

What is now uncovered, as well, is that either Meditation or Self-Hypnosis may be employed equally effectively, by either a Metaphysical Practitioner and/or Clinical Hypnotherapist, for improvement of one's outer self, potentially providing more services and flexibility , therefore, for the patient and/or Meditation-student.

Since Self-Hypnosis and Meditation have been shown, within the context of this essay, to be interchangeable in methodologies, brainwave-state and benefits, the title of this thesis, as well as the question, "Hypnosis or Meditation" have been realized and answered.

The only remaining issue that might persist in the mind of the Metaphysical Practitioner and/or Clinical Hypnotherapist, is not necessarily in the effectiveness of Meditation or Self-Hypnosis, but rather in that of their own competency in executing the methodologies. In addressing these personal doubts, we ask only that the regular and diligent practice and execution of Meditation and/or Self-Hypnosis be realized. As for the possible doubts as to the effectiveness of these modalities in actual and practical clinical or

Metaphysical practice, we ask only that the Metaphysician and/or Clinical Hypnotherapist attempt interchanging their use, either in their own private research, or in practical, clinical use, in their own practice, for the purposes of educating themselves and others as to the effectiveness of these modalities. Both Hypnosis and Meditation have been realized as practical tools.

▼

CHAPTER 3

The Human Brain from a Metaphysician's Perspective

The material for this chapter, originally from the Internet-film "Holographic Universe: Part 1 and 2" is included here for a number of reasons.

First, purely for entertainment value. It's interesting, above all.

Secondly, if you need to provide a scientific explanation for your patients and clients on how the senses are processed through the human brain, here it is.

Thirdly, it provides a Metaphysical perspective on the illusion of apparent "reality", for your interest, and for the interest and education of your clients and patients.

Fourth, it provides a quasi-scientific/logical explanation for the existence of "God".

Using the material in this chapter will allow for a different perspective on "reality", or the supposed illusion of "reality" and our senses. It could be used to show your patients and clients that what they have seen and experienced in the past isn't necessarily the "be all and end all", and therefore allow for a shift in attitude for them, ultimately resulting in their healing.

Beyond Matter

Man is conditioned from birth that the world he lives in has an absolute material reality. So he grows up under the effects of this conditioning and builds his entire life on this view-point. The findings of modern science, however, have revealed a completely different and significant reality than what is presumed.

All the information that we have about the external-world is conveyed to us by our five senses. The world we know of consists of what our eyes see, our ears hear, our noses smell, out tongues taste, and our hands feel.

Man is dependent on only those five senses, since birth.

That is why he knows the external-world only the way it is presented by these senses. Yet scientific research carried out on our senses has revealed very different facts about what we call "external-world", and these facts have brought to light a very important secret about matter which makes up the external-world.

Contemporary thinker Frederic Vester explains the point that science has reached on this subject: "Statements of some scientists posing that man is an image, everything experienced is temporary and deceptive, and this universe is a shadow, seems to be proven by science in our day."

In order to better grasp this secret behind matter, let us be reminded of our information about our sense of sight which provides us with the most extensive information about the external-world.

How Do We See?

The act of seeing is realized progressively: at the instance of seeing, light-clusters called photons travel from the object to the eye and pass through the eye's lenses where they are refracted and focus on the retina at the back of the eye. Here, rays are turned into electrical signals and then transmitted by neurons to the centre of vision, at the back of the brain.

The act of seeing actually takes place in this centre of the brain.

All the images we view in our lives, and all the events we experience, are actually experienced in this tiny and dark place. Both the words that you are now reading, and the boundless landscape that you see when you gaze at the horizon, actually fit into this place of a few cubic-centimetres.

Now let us reconsider this information more carefully.

When we say we see, we actually see the effect the rays reaching our eyes form in our brain by being converted into electric signals. When we say we see, we actually observe the electrical signals in our brain.

There is another point that has to be kept in mind: the brain is sealed to light, and its interior is absolutely dark. Therefore it is never possible for the brain to contact with light itself. We can explain this interesting situation with an example. Let us suppose that in front of us there is a burning candle, and we view its light. During this period when we view the candle's light, the inside of our skull and our brain are in absolute darkness. The light of the candle never illuminates our brain and our centre of vision; however, we watch a colorful and bright world inside our dark brain.

The same situation applies to all our other senses: sound, taste, touch, and smell are all perceived in the brain as electrical signals. Therefore our brains throughout our lives do not confront the original of the matter existing outside of us, but rather an electrical copy of it formed inside our brain. It is at this point that we are misled by assuming that these copies are instances of real matter outside us.

The External World Inside Our Brain

These physical facts make us come to an irrefutable conclusion: everything we see, hear, touch, feel, smell and perceive as matter, the world, or the universe, is only electrical signals inside our brain.

For instance, we see a bird in the external-world; in reality, this bird is not in the external-world, but in our brain. The light-particles reflecting from the bird reach our eye, and from there, they are converted into electrical-signals. These signals are transmitted by neurons to the centre of vision in the brain. The bird we see is in fact the electric signals in our brain. If the sight-nerves travelling to the brain were disconnected, the image of the bird would suddenly disappear. In the same manner, the bird's sounds we hear are also in our brain. If the nerve travelling from the ear to the brain was disconnected, there would be no sound left. Put simply, the bird, the shape of which we see, and the sound of which we hear, is nothing but the brain's interpretation of electrical signals.

Another point to be considered here is the sense of distance. For example, the distance between you and this book is nothing but a feeling of space formed in your brain. Also, objects that seem to be very distant in one person's view are actually images clustered at one spot in the brain. For instance, someone who watches the stars in the sky assumes that they are millions of light-years away from him, yet the stars are right inside himself, at the centre of vision, of his brain.

While you read this book, you are in truth not inside the room you assume yourself to be in; on the contrary: the room is inside you.

Your seeing your body makes you think you are inside of it, however, you must remember that your body too, is an image formed inside your brain.

So far, we have been speaking repeatedly of an external-world, and a world of perceptions formed in our brain, the latter of which is what we see; however, since we can never actually reach the external-world, how can we be sure that such a world really exists? Definitely we cannot. The only reality we cope with is the world of perceptions we live within our minds.

To imagine matter to have an existence outside the mind is indeed a deception. The perceptions we observe may well be coming from an artificial source. It is possible to see this in the mind's eye, by an example. First, let us suppose that we could take our brain out of our body, and keep it alive in a glass jar. Let us put a computer in, in which all kinds of information can be recorded. Finally let us transmit the electrical-signals of all the data related to a setting, such as image, sound, and smell, to this computer. Let us connect this computer to the sensory-centres in our brain with electrodes, and send the pre-recorded data to our brain. As our brain perceives these signals, it will see and live the settings correlated with these. From this computer, we can send to our brain also signals pertaining to our own image. For instance, we can send to our brain the electrical correlates of such senses as sight, hearing, and touch, that we perceive as we sit at a desk. In that state, our brain would think itself as a businessman sitting in his office. This imaginary-world would continue as long as the stimulations keep coming from the computer. We would never realize that we only consist of a brain. It is indeed very easy for us to be deceived into believing perceptions without any material correlates to be real. This is just what happens in our dreams.

The World in Dreams

For you, reality is all that can be touched with the hand and seen with the eye. In your dreams, you can also touch with your hand and see with your eye; but in reality, you have neither hand nor eye, nor is there anything that can be touched or seen. Taking what you perceive in your dream to be material realities, you are simply deceived. For example, a person deeply-asleep in his bed may see himself in an entirely different world in his dream: he may dream that he is a pilot and command a giant airplane, and even spend a great effort to command the plane. In fact, this person has not taken even one step away from his bed. In his dreams, he may visit different settings and meet with friends, have a chat with them, eat, and drink together. It is only when the person awakes from his dream that he realizes all were only perceptions.

If we are able to live easily in an unreal world during our dreams, the same thing can equally be true for the world we live in. When we wake up from a dream, there is no logical reason for not thinking that we have entered a longer dream that we call "real-life". The reason we consider our dream to be fantasy, and the world as real, is nothing but a product of our habits and prejudices.

This suggests that we may well be awoken from a life on earth which we think we are living right now, just as we are awoken from a dream.

Who is The Perceiver?

After all these physical facts arises the question of primary importance: if all physical events that we know are intrinsically perceptions, what about our brain? Since our brain is matter just like our arms, legs, or any other object, it also must be a perception, just like all other objects.

An example will illuminate this subject further. Let us think we extend a nerve reaching our brain, and put it outside our head, where we can see it with our eyes. In this case, we would also be able to see our brain, and touch it with our fingers. This way, we can understand that our brain is also nothing but a perception formed by the senses of vision and touch.

Then, what is the will that sees, hears, and perceives all other senses if it is not the brain? Who is it that sees, hears, touches, and perceives the tastes and smells? Who is this being that thinks, reasons, has feelings, and moreover that says "I am me"? One of the important thinkers of our age, Ken Wilber poses the same question: "Since the Greeks, Philosophers have been thinking about the "ghost in the machine"; the "small man within the small man", etc. Where is "I", the person who uses his brain? Who is it that realizes the act of "knowing"?"

St. Francis of Assisi said, "What we search for is the One that sees."

In fact, this Metaphysical-being that uses the brain, that sees and feels, is the soul. What we call the material-world is the aggregate of perceptions viewed and felt by this soul. Just as the bodies we possess, and the material-world we see in our dreams have no physical-reality, the universe we occupy, and the bodies we possess now also have no physical-reality. The real, absolute-being, is the soul. Matter consists merely of perceptions viewed by the soul. Yes, even if we start with the presupposition that matter is real, the laws of physics, chemistry, and biology all lead us to the fact that matter consists of an illusion, and to the inevitable actuality of a Metaphysical matter.

This is the secret beyond matter; this fact is so definite, that it alarms some materialist-scientists, who think matter to be the absolute-being.

Science-writer Lincoln Barnett says in his book "The Universe and Einstein", "Along with Philosophers' reduction of all objective-reality to a shadow-world of perceptions, scientists have become aware of the alarming limitations of man's senses."

All these facts bring us face-to-face with a very significant question: if the thing we acknowledge to be the material-world is merely comprised of perceptions given to our soul, then what is the source of these perceptions? In answering this question, we must consider the fact that matter does not have a self-governing existence by itself but it is a perception. Therefore, this perception must have been caused by another power, which means that it must have been created. Moreover, this creation must be continuous. If there were not a consistent and continuous creation, then what we call matter would disappear and be lost. This may be likened to a television, on which a picture is displayed, as long as the signal continues to be broadcast. If the broadcast stops, the image on the screen will also disappear.

The Real Absolute Being

So, who makes our soul see the earth, people, plants, our bodies, and all else that we see? It is very evident that there is a superior creator who has created the entire material universe: that is, the sum of all perceptions, and continues his creation ceaselessly. Since this creator displays such a magnificent creation, he surely has eternal power and might; all the perceptions he creates are dependent on his will, and he dominates everything he has created at any moment.

PART 3

TOOLS FOR SELF-ASSESSMENT

CHAPTER I

▼

The Four Temperaments

I would be remiss at this point if I did not include several tools both for self-assessment and the assessment of others' personality types. Phineas Parkhurst Quimby used this ancient concept as a starting point for the transformation and healing of his patients.

Today, the principles behind the Four Temperaments form the basis for personality analysis, and even help to determine whether a potential employee will be hired or not.

Throughout history there have been many attempts to explain why people are different. One of the first systems developed was Astrology, which looked outside of man to explain the differences. There were twelve "signs" symbolized by earth, air, fire and water. Hippocrates (470?-360? B.C.), however, looked inside of man to explain the differences. He believed that behavior was determined by the presence of an excessive amount of one of four fluids or humors; *yellow bile* (Chlor); *red bile* or blood (Sangis); *white bile* (Phlegm); *black bile* (Melan). These four humors were thought to be related to the four elements of earth, air, fire and water. Hippocrates, and other early Greeks, thought that an excess of one of the four humors produced a particular temperament and behavior.

The word "temperament" comes from the Latin word *temperamentum* and means "right blending." The Greeks thought that a person's "temperament" was therefore made up of a blending of these four fluids.

An excess of **yellow bile** resulted in a temperament believed to be warm/hot and dry, and associated with the element of fire [Choleric].

An excess of **red bile** resulted in a temperament believed to be warm/hot and wet, and associated with the element of air [Sanguine].

An excess of **white bile** resulted in a temperament believed to be cool/cold and wet, and associated with the element of water [Phlegmatic].

An excess of **black bile** resulted in a temperament believed to be cool/cold and dry, and associated with the element of earth [Melancholy].

Hippocrates and the early Greeks were accurate in their observations of behavior but were incorrect about the origin of these tendencies (they are not created by the excess of a fluid). Today we would say that they originate from some genetic predisposition, although we cannot be certain.

Galen (129?-203?) was a Greek physician, who lived 600 years after Hippocrates and was responsible for popularizing the temperaments during his time and relating them to illness. He is credited with coining the terms, Choleric, Sanguine, Phlegmatic and Melancholy.

Immual Kant (1724-1804) described the four temperaments in his book, Anthropology from a Pragmatic Point of View, 1798.

Nicholas Culpeper (1616-1654) was the first to dispute two fundamental concepts that had existed since the time of Hippocrates. First, he rejected the idea that the four "humors" were the cause of a person's temperament. Secondly, he was the first to say that a person is influenced by two temperaments, one primary and one secondary. Before Culpeper, it was believed that a person had only one temperament.

William M. Marston (1893-1947) was the first to contribute scientific evidence that people fit into one of four categories. He published Emotions of Normal People in 1928 using the terms: Dominant, Influence, Steadiness and Compliance. Marston studied the emotions of normal people because research had centered around the emotions of abnormal people during his era. He observed behavior and identified thirty-five words or phrases that characterized four people according to their emotional response to a favorable and unfavorable situation. A little known fact is that Marston was responsible for the invention of the systolic blood-pressure test which led to the creation of the lie detector. He also created the cartoon character, Wonder Woman.

Ole Halsbey contributed penetrating insight into the behavior of the four temperaments in his book, Temperament And The Christian Faith, in the 1930's using the terms, Choleric, Sanguine, Phlegmatic and Melancholy.

John G. Geier built on the works of William M. Marston (1928), Walter Clarke (1940) and John Cleaver (1950). Walter Clarke developed the Activity Vector Analysis using the four dimensions of Aggressive, Sociable, Stable and Avoidant. John Cleaver created a 24 question forced-choice instrument from the work of Walter Clarke.

John Geier, building on the works of Marston, Cleaver and Clark, was the first to develop (by factor analysis) an instrument that identified an individual's behavioral style (temperament blend) and identified 15 classical patterns. These are patterns that frequently reoccurred on his instrument. Dr. Geier developed the Personal Profile System instrument in 1958 and eventually formed the company Performax to market the materials to the business community (early 1960's). His DiSC profile enabled business companies to build a more effective team and match a person's natural tendencies to a specific task. He used the terms: High "D" (Dominant); High "i" (Influencing); High "S" (Steadiness); and High "C" (Competent).

Tim LaHaye was the first to popularize the concept to the Christian community. Dr. LaHaye published the first of several books in the late 1970's using the terms, Choleric, Sanguine, Phlegmatic and Melancholy.

Hans J. Eysenck wrote Personality and Individual Differences, A Natural Science Approach, in 1985. Dr. Eysenck has written other books on the subject including, The Biological Basis of Personality (1967).

Others have contributed to the temperament model of behavior, using different terms, including, Plato (350 BC), Paracelsus (1530), Adickes (1905), Spranger (1914), Kretschmer (1930), Adler (1937), Fromm (1947), Myers (1955) and Keirsey (1970).

Summary

The ancient Greeks observed people and speculated on the reasons for their behavior. Their observations were supported in   later centuries by a wide variety of people including physicians and philosophers. In the early 1900's the scientific method was applied by Marston with the same results. The concept has been observed for centuries and verified by science that people fall into four categories, and everyone describes the four basically the same.

Correlation of Terms

There have been many different terms used to refer to the four temperaments. Below is a correlation of some the more popular ones:

Choleric	Sanguine	Phlegmatic	Melancholy
Dominant	Influencing	Steadiness	Compliance
High "D"	High "i"	High "S"	High "C"
Directive	Interactive	Supportive	Corrective
Driver	Expressive	Amiable	Analytical
Red	Yellow	Gray	Blue

Description of the 4 Primary Temperaments

According to John T. Cocoris, the following is an overview description of the four primary temperaments.

The "Choleric" is an extroverted, hot-tempered, quick thinking, active, practical, strong-willed and easily annoyed person. Cholerics are self-confident, self-sufficient and very independent minded. They are decisive and opinionated and find it easy to make decisions for themselves as well as others. Cholerics tend to leave little room for negotiating. The Choleric is a visionary and seems to never run out of ideas, plans and goals, which are usually very practical. The Choleric does not require as much sleep as the other temperaments so their activity seems endless. Their activity almost always has a purpose because they are by nature result-oriented. They usually do not give in to the pressure of what others think unless they see that they cannot get the desired results. Cholerics can be crusaders against social injustice as they love to fight for a cause. Cholerics are both direct and firm when responding to others. They are slow to build relationships because results tend to be more important than people. They do not easily empathize with the feelings of others or show compassion. Cholerics think big and seek positions of authority.

The "Sanguine" is an extroverted, fun-loving, activity-prone, impulsive, entertaining, persuasive, easily amused and optimistic person. Sanguines are receptive and open to others and build relationships quickly. They are animated, excited and accepting of others. They will smile and talk easily and often. It is not unusual to feel as if you have known the Sanguine person for years after only a few minutes. Sanguines are so people-oriented that they easily forget about time and are often late arriving at their destination. Sanguines get bored easily because of their orientation to social involvement, activity and general dislike for solitude. The Sanguine never lacks for friends. Their attention span is based on whether or not they are interested in the person or event. The Sanguine can change their focus or interest in an instant. Sanguines are competitive and tend to be disorganized. Unless very disciplined, the Sanguine will have difficulty controlling their emotions. They usually like sports of any kind because of the activity and involvement with other people. Their voice will show excitement and friendliness. Sanguines usually dress according to current fashion. The Sanguine fears rejection or not making a favorable impression. They also fear others viewing them as unsuccessful. Sanguines are very effective working with people.

The "Phlegmatic" is an introverted, calm, unemotional, easygoing, never-get-upset, person. Phlegmatics are both slow and indirect when responding to others. They are also slow to warm-up but will be accommodating in the process. Phlegmatics are by far the easiest person with which to get along. They live a quiet, routine life, free of the normal anxieties and stresses of the other temperaments. The Phlegmatic will avoid getting too involved with people and life in general. Phlegmatics seldom exert themselves with others or push their way along in their career, they just let it happen. The Phlegmatic communicates a warm, sincere interest in others preferring to have just a few close friends. They will be very loyal to their friends and find it difficult to break long standing relationships regardless of what the other person does. The Phlegmatic tends to resist change of any kind without reason, other than they just do not want the change to occur. Phlegmatics show little emotion and are prone to be a grudge holder. Phlegmatics tend to avoid conflict and making decisions of any kind. They are practical, concrete and traditional thinkers. Their stoic expression often hides their true feelings. The Phlegmatic may be patient to the point of paralysis. Phlegmatics are persistent and consistent at whatever they undertake.

The "Melancholy" is an introverted, logical, analytical, factual, private, lets-do-it-right person. Melancholies respond to others in a slow, cautious and indirect manner. Melancholies are reserved and suspicious until sure of your intentions. The Melancholy probe for the "hidden meaning" behind your words. They are timid and may appear unsure and have a serious expression. They are self-sacrificing, gifted and they tend to be a perfectionist. Melancholies are very sensitive to what others think about their work. The Melancholy is well organized; on occasion you may find a Melancholy that keeps things cluttered, however, they know what's in the piles. The Melancholy is determined to make the right and best decision. Melancholies will ask specific questions and sometimes they will ask the same question again and again. The Melancholy needs reassurance, feedback and reasons why they should do something. They need information, time to think and a plan. The Melancholy fears taking a risk, making a wrong decision and being viewed as incompetent. Melancholies tend to have a negative attitude toward something new until they have had time to think it over. Melancholies are skeptical about most everything but they are creative and capable people. Melancholies tend to get bored with something once they get it figured out.

Descriptions of The 15 Temperament Blends

These, again, are according to John T. Cocoris, Psy.D.

Choleric (High "D") Blends

1. Executive Pattern
Choleric-Sanguine
("D-I")

The Executive tends to be very impatient and will often take a win/lose approach to life. They are practical and use direct methods to get quick results but still show an interest in people. They are goal and bottom line oriented and can be very persuasive in promoting their ideas. They want to be in charge because of confidence in their ability to make decisions. They have boundless energy and need activity and results or they become bored. They need daily challenge and others willing to listen to them and carry out their plans. This versatile, eager, self-starter is very competitive. To be highly motivated they need freedom, the opportunity for advancement and information that will help them get results. They like having power and authority. The Choleric fights for what they think is the right way to accomplish the goal but they can accept momentary defeat and tend not to be grudge holders. They dislike weakness.

2. Motivator Pattern
Choleric-Sanguine
("D-I")

The Motivator tends to be very impatient and will often take a win/lose approach to life. They are practical and use direct, sometimes forceful methods to get quick results but still show some interest in people. They are goal and bottom line oriented and can be very forceful in promoting their ideas. They want to be in charge because of confidence in their ability to make decisions. They have boundless energy and need activity and results or they become bored. They need daily challenge and others willing to listen to them and carry out their plans. This versatile, eager, self-starter is very competitive. To be highly motivated they need freedom, the opportunity for advancement and information that will help them get results. They like having power and authority. The Choleric fights for what they think is the right way to accomplish the goal, but they can accept momentary defeat and tend not to be grudge holders. They dislike weakness.

3. Director Pattern
Choleric-Phlegmatic
("D-S")

The Director is more determined, unemotional and individualistic than the other Cholerics. They are very practical. They will use very direct and persistent methods to get results or promote their ideas. They want to be in charge because of confidence in their ability to make decisions. They usually have deep personal goals and may pursue them at the expense of the organization. They need to know the "big picture" (clear direction) before they can function efficiently. They tend to have difficulty working with others because of their independent nature and lack of natural people-skills. To be highly motivated they need freedom, independence, the opportunity for advancement and information that will help them get quick results. They dislike weakness.

4. Strategist Pattern
Choleric-Melancholy
("D-C")

The Strategist is more detail oriented than the other Cholerics. They initiate change. They usually operate from a well-thought through plan. They have creative ideas. They will often use very direct, forceful and persistent methods to get results or promote their ideas. They want to be in charge because of confidence in their ability to make things happen the "right" way. They like to solve problems and make decisions¾and are actually quite able to do so. They usually have well thought-out goals and are very independent in an attempt to carry them out. They need to know exactly what is expected before they can function efficiently. They can be very forceful and very sensitive. They speak with authority and are usually very productive. When working on a project they exhibit sensitivity and strategy that reveals penetrating insight. To be highly motivated they need freedom, the opportunity for advancement, information that will help them get results and the chance to make something better. They dislike weakness.

Sanguine (High "I") Blends

5. Negotiator Pattern
Sanguine-Choleric
("I-D")

The Negotiator is more assertive than the other Sanguines. They easily manipulate others. They are very energetic and work well with and through people. This person has an outgoing interest in others and the ability to gain the respect and confidence of varied types of individuals. They strive to do business in a friendly way while pushing forward to win objectives and sell their point of view. They are able to coordinate events and the are willing to delegate responsibilities. They exhibit poise and confidence in most situations, especially social events. They will become bored without activity and social involvement. They have a difficult time with details, organization and consistency. They prefer others to give them information that will help them make decisions rather than research it themselves. They work very well with others and make good leaders. They are very optimistic but lack follow through. To be highly motivated they need freedom of expression, recognition, involvement with people, acceptance and freedom from details.

6. Marketer Pattern
Sanguine-Choleric
("I-D")

The Marketer is more enthusiastic than the other Sanguines. They get very excited. This is an assertive and energetic persons who works well with and through people. They have an outgoing interest in others and the ability to gain the respect and confidence of varied types of individuals. They strive to do business in a friendly way while pushing forward to win their objectives and sell their point of view. They easily promote their own ideas or the ideas of others. They exhibit poise and confidence in most situations, especially social events. They will become bored without activity and social involvement. They have difficulty with awareness of time, organization and concentrating on details. They prefer others to give them information that will help them make decisions rather than research it themselves. They are very optimistic and enthusiastic but lack consistent follow-through. To be highly motivated they need freedom of expression, mobility, involvement with people, recognition, acceptance and freedom from details.

7. Relater Pattern
Sanguine-Phlegmatic
("I-S")

The Relater is more relationship oriented than the other Sanguines. They are very approachable and place high importance on enduring relationships. This person impresses most people with their warmth, empathy and understanding approach. They possess a casual kind of poise in social situations. People tend to seek them out to share their problems because they perceive them to be a good listener. Children especially like them. Although doing details and organizational things give them difficulty, they are able to do them. They work very well with others. They are optimistic and accommodating. To be highly motivated they need freedom of expression, the opportunity to build relationships and to be of service to others.

8. Performer Pattern
Sanguine-Melancholy
("I-C")

The Performer is more formal than the other Sanguines. They are very concerned about making a favorable impression and being accepted by others. They tend to be very image conscious and tend to actively seek recognition for their achievements. They are usually well organized but may not be consistent or follow-through. Information about their job is very important to them so they may ask many questions. They function best when they have a detailed plan. To be highly motivated they need security, freedom of expression, relationships with people and the opportunity to be creative. They also need information, time to think and a plan before they can function effectively. They may be reluctant to take action until they have confidence that they will not fail. If they cannot be sure, they often do not try.

Phlegmatic (High "S") Blends

9. Inspector Pattern
Phlegmatic-Choleric
("S-D")

The Inspector is more industrious, determined and unemotional than the other Phlegmatics. This persistent individual brings a deceptively intense approach to the task. Being low-key outwardly, their involvement in a task is not easily observed. They are a dispassionate "anchor of reality." They are calm, steady and persevering. They are successful because of dogged determination. After starting a project they are tenacious and will fight hard for their objectives. They are very independent, questioning and thorough in their approach and will follow through. They want to operate by themselves and set their own pace. Once their mind is made up they will resist any other method of approach; they can be very stubborn! They seek challenging assignments without close supervision. They prefer work of a technical nature rather than involvement with people.

10. Harmonizer Pattern
Phlegmatic-Sanguine
("S-I")

The Harmonizer is more friendly than the other Phlegmatics. They are very accepting and tolerant of others. This person is very accommodating and easy to be associated with in the work environment and as a friend. They need some social involvement. They are loyal, consistent and dependable. They will often work when they are ill. They are very independent minded and want to operate by themselves and set their own pace. They learn by doing. Once their mind is made up they will resist any other method of approach. They can do routine work but will need some activity during the day. They have a very difficult time saying no and will often take on more than they can do. They have a very pleasant, soft voice.

11. Helper Pattern
Phlegmatic-Melancholy
("S-C")

The Helper is more consistent than the other Phlegmatics. They are very routine, accommodating and passive. Patience, control and deliberateness characterize the usual behavior of this amiable and easy going individual. This determined and persistent individual brings a deceptively intense approach to the task. Being low-key, their involvement in a task is not easily observed. They are calm, steady and persevering. They are successful because of persistence. After starting a project they will usually see it through to completion. They are independent, questioning and thorough in their approach and will follow through. They want to operate by themselves and set their own pace. They are very possessive of family, material things and friends. Once their mind is made up they will resist any other method of approach. They prefer work of a technical nature and involvement with a limited number of people. They approach a task with calculated moderation. They are always willing to help those they consider to be their friend.

Melancholy (High "C") Blends

12. Trainer Pattern
Melancholy-Choleric
("C-D")

The Trainer is more forceful than the other Melancholies. They are systematic, precise thinkers and follow procedures in both their business and personal life. They are attentive to detail and push to have things done correctly, according to their own predetermined standards. They are sensitive and conscientious. They normally behave in a diplomatic manner except when it comes to deviating from standards they have accepted. They can then be very forceful in insisting the right way be followed. They are not socially active, preferring work and privacy to people. They tend to have difficulty in relationships because they are not flexible and they can be abrasive when communicating with others. They make decisions slowly because of collecting and analyzing information until they are sure of the best course of action. To be highly motivated they need a structured environment with clear rules and procedures, time to organize, collect information, think and the freedom to develop a plan.

13. Idealist Pattern
Melancholy-Phlegmatic-Choleric
("C-S-D")

The Idealist is unique because the Choleric temperament has strong influence on their behavior. The combination of Melancholy-Phlegmatic-Choleric urges this person to "push" their ideal standards to perfection.

The Idealist is a systematic, precise thinker and will follow procedures in both their business and personal life. They are attentive to detail and push to have things done correctly, according to predetermined standards (usually their own). They are conscientious in work requiring accuracy and maintaining high, sometimes unrealistic, standards. They normally behave in a diplomatic manner except when it comes to deviating from standards they have accepted. They can then be very forceful in insisting the "right way" be followed. They are not socially active, preferring privacy. They tend to have difficulty in relationships because they are rigid and maintain high standards. They make decisions slowly because of collecting and analyzing information until they are sure of the best course of action. To be highly motivated they need a structured environment with clear rules and procedures, time to organize, collect information, think and the freedom to develop a plan.

14. Diplomat Pattern
Melancholy-Sanguine
("C-I")

The Diplomat is more friendly than the other Melancholy blends. They have high personal ambitions. This is a well-balanced systematic, precise thinker and worker who tends to follow procedures in both their business and personal life. They are attentive to detail and friendly. They like to do things correctly, according to predetermined standards. They are extremely conscientious. They need some mobility, rather then sitting for long periods of time. This is a versatile, productive individual that works well with most everyone. At times they can be sensitive, especially to criticism. They make decisions slowly because of collecting and analyzing information until they are sure of the best course of action (this is especially true when involved in a new project). To be highly motivated they need a structured environment with clear rules and procedures, time to organize, collect information, think and time to develop a plan and have some social interaction.

15. Analyst Pattern
Melancholy-Phlegmatic
("C-S")

The Analyst is more conscientious and private than the other Melancholy blends. They withdraw from aggressive people. This quite individual works well in a structured environment requiring attention to detail. They are a systematic, precise thinker and worker who tends to follow procedures in both their business and personal life. They make decisions slowly because of collecting and analyzing information until they are sure of the *right* and *best* course of action (this is especially true when involved in a new project). They are good at anticipating problems but not good at taking action. They are usually very well organized and function best when they have a well-through out plan. To be highly motivated they need a structured environment with clear rules and procedures, time to organize, collect information, think and the time to develop a plan.

Overview of Keirsey's Four Temperaments

According to David Keirsey, Ph.D., Temperament is a configuration of observable personality traits, such as habits of communication, patterns of action, and sets of characteristic attitudes, values, and talents. It also encompasses personal needs, the kinds of contributions that individuals make in the workplace, and the roles they play in society. Dr. David Keirsey has identified mankind's four basic temperaments as the Artisan, the Guardian, the Rational, and the Idealist.

Each temperament has its own unique qualities and shortcomings, strengths and challenges. What accounts for these differences? To use the idea of Temperament most effectively, it is important to understand that the four temperaments are not simply arbitrary collections of characteristics, but spring from an interaction of the two basic dimensions of human behavior: our communication and our action, our words and our deeds, or, simply, what we say and what we do.

Communication: Concrete vs. Abstract

First, people naturally think and talk about what they are interested in, and if you listen carefully to people's conversations, you find two broad but distinct areas of subject matter.

Some people talk primarily about the external, concrete world of everyday reality: facts and figures, work and play, home and family, news, sports and weather -- all the who-what-when-where-and how much's of life.

Other people talk primarily about the internal, abstract world of ideas: theories and conjectures, dreams and philosophies, beliefs and fantasies --all the why's, if's, and what-might-be's of life.

At times, of course, everyone addresses both sorts of topics, but in their daily lives, and for the most part, Concrete people talk about reality, while Abstract people talk about ideas.

Action: Utilitarian vs. Cooperative

Second, at every turn people are trying to accomplish their goals, and if you watch closely how people go about their business, you see that there are two fundamentally opposite types of action.

Some people act primarily in a utilitarian or pragmatic manner, that is, they do what gets results, what achieves their objectives as effectively or efficiently as possible, and only afterwards do they check to see if they are observing the rules or going through proper channels.

Other people act primarily in a cooperative or socially acceptable manner, that is, they try to do the right thing, in keeping with agreed upon social rules, conventions, and codes of conduct, and only later do they concern themselves with the effectiveness of their actions.

These two ways of acting can overlap, certainly, but as they lead their lives, Utilitarian people instinctively, and for the most part, do what works, while Cooperative people do what's right.

- As Concrete Cooperators, Guardians speak mostly of their duties and responsibilities, of what they can keep an eye on and take good care of, and they're careful to obey the laws, follow the rules, and respect the rights of others.

- As Abstract Cooperators, Idealists speak mostly of what they hope for and imagine might be possible for people, and they want to act in good conscience, always trying to reach their goals without compromising their personal code of ethics.

- As Concrete Utilitarians, Artisans speak mostly about what they see right in front of them, about what they can get their hands on, and they will do whatever works, whatever gives them a quick, effective payoff, even if they have to bend the rules.

- As Abstract Utilitarians, Rationals speak mostly of what new problems intrigue them and what new solutions they envision, and always pragmatic, they act as efficiently as possible to achieve their objectives, ignoring arbitrary rules and conventions if need be.

Guardians

All Guardians (SJs) share the following core characteristics:

Guardians pride themselves on being dependable, helpful, and hard-working.

Guardians make loyal mates, responsible parents, and stabilizing leaders.

Guardians tend to be dutiful, cautious, humble, and focused on credentials and traditions.

Guardians are concerned citizens who trust authority, join groups, seek security, prize gratitude, and dream of meting out justice.

Guardians are the cornerstone of society, for they are the temperament given to serving and preserving our most important social institutions. Guardians have natural talent in managing goods and services--from supervision to maintenance and supply -- and they use all their skills to keep things running smoothly in their families, communities, schools, churches, hospitals, and businesses.

Guardians can have a lot of fun with their friends, but they are quite serious about their duties and responsibilities. Guardians take pride in being dependable and trustworthy; if there's a job to be done, they can be counted on to put their shoulder to the wheel.

Guardians also believe in law and order, and sometimes worry that respect for authority, even a fundamental sense of right and wrong, is being lost. Perhaps this is why Guardians honor customs and traditions so strongly -- they are familiar patterns that help bring stability to our modern, fast-paced world.

Practical and down-to-earth, Guardians believe in following the rules and cooperating with others. They are not very comfortable winging it or blazing new trails; working steadily within the system is the Guardian way, for in the long run loyalty, discipline, and teamwork get the job done right. Guardians are meticulous about schedules and have a sharp eye for proper procedures. They are cautious about change, even though they know that change can be healthy for an institution. Better to go slowly, they say, and look before you leap.

Guardians make up as much as 40 to 45 percent of the population, and a good thing, because they usually end up doing all the indispensable but thankless jobs the rest of us take for granted.

Presidents George Washington, Harry S. Truman, William Howard Taft and Mother Teresa are examples of Guardians.

Idealists

All Idealists (NFs) share the following core characteristics:

Idealists are enthusiastic, they trust their intuition, yearn for romance, seek their true self, prize meaningful relationships, and dream of attaining wisdom.

Idealists pride themselves on being loving, kindhearted, and authentic.

Idealists tend to be giving, trusting, spiritual, and they are focused on personal journeys and human potentials.

Idealists make intense mates, nurturing parents, and inspirational leaders.

Idealists, as a temperament, are passionately concerned with personal growth and development. Idealists strive to discover who they are and how they can become their best possible self -- always this quest for self-knowledge and self-improvement drives their imagination. And they want to help others make the journey. Idealists are naturally drawn to working with people, and whether in education or counseling, in social services or personnel work, in journalism or the ministry, they are gifted at helping others find their way in life, often inspiring them to grow as individuals and to fulfill their potentials.

Idealists are sure that friendly cooperation is the best way for people to achieve their goals. Conflict and confrontation upset them because they seem to put up angry barriers between people. Idealists dream of creating harmonious, even caring personal relations, and they have a unique talent for helping people get along with each other and work together for the good of all. Such interpersonal harmony might be a romantic ideal, but then Idealists are incurable romantics who prefer to focus on what might be, rather than what is. The real, practical world is only a starting place for Idealists; they believe that life is filled with possibilities waiting to be realized, rich with meanings calling out to be understood. This idea of a mystical or spiritual dimension to life, the "not visible" or the "not yet" that can only be known through intuition or by a leap of faith, is far more important to Idealists than the world of material things.

Highly ethical in their actions, Idealists hold themselves to a strict standard of personal integrity. They must be true to themselves and to others, and they can be quite hard on themselves when they are dishonest, or when they are false or insincere. More often, however, Idealists are the very soul of kindness. Particularly in their personal relationships, Idealists are without question filled with love and good will. They believe in giving of themselves to help others; they cherish a few warm, sensitive friendships; they strive for a special rapport with their children; and in marriage they wish to find a "soulmate," someone with whom they can bond emotionally and spiritually, sharing their deepest feelings and their complex inner worlds.

Idealists are relatively rare, making up no more than 15 to 20 percent of the population. But their ability to inspire people with their enthusiasm and their idealism has given them influence far beyond their numbers.

Princess Diana, Joan Baez, Albert Schweitzer, Bill Moyers, Eleanor Roosevelt, Mohandas Gandhi, Mikhael Gorbachev, and Oprah Winfrey are examples of Idealists.

Artisans

All Artisans (SPs) share the following core characteristics:

Artisans tend to be fun-loving, optimistic, realistic, and focused on the here and now

Artisans pride themselves on being unconventional, bold, and spontaneous.

Artisans make playful mates, creative parents, and troubleshooting leaders.

Artisans are excitable, trust their impulses, want to make a splash, seek stimulation, prize freedom, and dream of mastering action skills.

Artisans are the temperament with a natural ability to excel in any of the arts, not only the fine arts such as painting and sculpting, or the performing arts such as music, theater, and dance, but also the athletic, military, political, mechanical, and industrial arts, as well as the "art of the deal" in business.

Artisans are most at home in the real world of solid objects that can be made and manipulated, and of real-life events that can be experienced in the here and now. Artisans have exceptionally keen senses, and love working with their hands. They seem right at home with tools, instruments, and vehicles of all kinds, and their actions are usually aimed at getting them where they want to go, and as quickly as possible. Thus Artisans will strike off boldly down roads that others might consider risky or impossible, doing whatever it takes, rules or no rules, to accomplish their goals. This devil-may-care attitude also gives the Artisans a winning way with people, and they are often irresistibly charming with family, friends, and co-workers.

Artisans want to be where the action is; they seek out adventure and show a constant hunger for pleasure and stimulation. They believe that variety is the spice of life, and that doing things that aren't fun or exciting is a waste of time. Artisans are impulsive, adaptable, competitive, and believe the next throw of the dice will be the lucky one. They can also be generous to a fault, always ready to share with their friends from the bounty of life. Above all, Artisans need to be free to do what they wish, when they wish. They resist being tied or bound or confined or obligated; they would rather not wait, or save, or store, or live for tomorrow. In the Artisan view, today must be enjoyed, for tomorrow never comes.

There are many Artisans, perhaps 30 to 35 percent of the population, which is good, because they create much of the beauty, grace, fun, and excitement the rest of us enjoy in life.

Ernest Hemingway, Franklin Delano Roosevelt, Bruce Lee, Amelia Earhart, Bob Dylan, Barbra Streisand, Elvis Presley, Elizabeth Taylor, Madonna, and President John F. Kennedy are examples of Artisans.

The Rationals

All Rationals (NTs) share the following core characteristics:

Rationals tend to be pragmatic, skeptical, self-contained, and focused on problem-solving and systems analysis.

Rationals pride themselves on being ingenious, independent, and strong willed.

Rationals make reasonable mates, individualizing parents, and strategic leaders.

Rationals are even-tempered, they trust logic, yearn for achievement, seek knowledge, prize technology, and dream of understanding how the world works.

Rationals are the problem solving temperament, particularly if the problem has to do with the many complex systems that make up the world around us. Rationals might tackle problems in organic systems such as plants and animals, or in mechanical systems such as railroads and computers, or in social systems such as families and companies and governments. But whatever systems fire their curiosity, Rationals will analyze them to understand how they work, so they can figure out how to make them work better.

In working with problems, Rationals try to find solutions that have application in the real world, but they are even more interested in the abstract concepts involved, the fundamental principles or natural laws that underlie the particular case. And they are completely pragmatic about their ways and means of achieving their ends. Rationals don't care about being politically correct. They are interested in the most efficient solutions possible, and will listen to anyone who has something useful to teach them, while disregarding any authority or customary procedure that wastes time and resources.

Rationals have an insatiable hunger to accomplish their goals and will work tirelessly on any project they have set their mind to. They are rigorously logical and fiercely independent in their thinking -- are indeed skeptical of all ideas, even their own -- and they believe they can overcome any obstacle with their will power. Often they are seen as cold and distant, but this is really the absorbed concentration they give to whatever problem they're working on. Whether designing a skyscraper or an experiment, developing a theory or a prototype technology, building an aircraft, a corporation, or a strategic alliance, Rationals value intelligence, in themselves and others, and they pride themselves on the ingenuity they bring to their problem solving.

Rationals are very scarce, comprising as little as 5 to 10 percent of the population. But because of their drive to unlock the secrets of nature, and to develop new technologies, they have done much to shape our world.

Albert Einstein, Marie Curie, Bill Gates, Margaret Thatcher, Walt Disney, Camille Paglia, Ayn Rand, Thomas Jefferson, Richard Feynman, and General Ulysses S. Grant and President Dwight D. Eisenhower are examples of Rationals.

Conclusion

It was my sincere desire in outlining these unique methods of personality analysis, to give you greater insight into yourself, and your friends, family, and patients.

The more insight we have into people, the better our chances of helping them to help themselves.

▼

CHAPTER 2

Mind-Treatments

To truly honor the rich heritage of Phineas Parkhurst Quimby's legacy, I have decided to include at this point a lecture given in 1887 by Julius A. Dresser.

Julius and Annetta Dresser: A Brief Biography

Julius and Annetta Dresser were early practitioners of the healing methods taught and practiced by <u>Phineas Parkhurst Quimby</u>. Julius A. Dresser was born February 12, 1838, in Portland, Maine. He had intended entering the ministry in the Calvinistic Baptist church, and was studying in Waterville College, Maine, when his health failed. Hearing of P. P. Quimby as a healer, and thinking he had not long to live, he went to him and in a short time was healed. This was in 1860. 1862 was the year that Mary Patterson (Mary Baker Eddy), who later founded the Christian Science church, first visited Dr. Quimby for healing.

At Dr. Quimby's office Julius met Annetta Seabury, who also came seeking health, and in 1863 the two were married. Julius Dresser became an enthusiastic advocate of Quimby's system and devoted himself to explaining it to others. He had become editor of a Portland newspaper in 1866, but moved to Webster, Massachusetts, where he became editor and publisher of the *Webster Times*. This same year Annetta gave birth to their first son, Horatio, who went on to become a prolific author of New Thought books.

1866 was also the year that Dr. Quimby died, and shortly afterwards Mrs. Patterson fell one day on the ice and suffered a serious injury. She felt lost without Quimby's sustaining healing power and wrote to Julius Dresser urging that he take up the work and try to heal her. He refused to take up the responsibility, however, and a little later moved West and lived there several years.

Returning to Massachusetts, he and his wife took up the practice of mental healing in Boston in 1882. The Dressers had no public meetings at first, but only personal contact with individuals seeking to be healed. They operated strictly on the basis of the Quimby principles. When in 1883 they began teaching classes, it was the Quimby system they taught, encouraged to do so by seeing pupils of Mrs. Eddy and some she had rejected practicing and doing what the Dressers considered to be work inferior to that of Quimby. They made use of the Quimby manuscripts in their teaching. Thus the teachings of Quimby and Mary Baker Eddy were set in contrast and the so-called Quimby controversy began.

In 1884 the Dressers issued a circular setting forth their theories and methods, which closely followed Dr. Quimby's ideas and method. Answering various questions concerning their method they assert that it is not that of any of the "isms" of the day, but rather "a purely mental treatment, and its results are a triumph of mind over the ills of suffering humanity, and of the real truth of a sick person's case over the opinions that assume to know."

They make no use of medicines or other material means. It is, they assert, "natural and right to be well, and the simple truth understood and applied destroys the error of disease." Their examinations are by mental perceptions (intuition) which reveal the nature of the disease. In this and the method of cure they are following out specifically "the principles of truth discovered and reduced to a science by Mr. P. P. Quimby of Maine. They had learned it from him personally, and knew no other name for it than "The Quimby System of Mental Treatment of Diseases." The system might properly be called a Spiritual Science, and must be judged only by its fruits.

They were successful in their healing practice. People who were healed wanted to know by what means the healing was wrought. Instead of writing it down and letting patients read it as Dr. Quimby had done, the Dressers held classes, giving instruction through lectures. Generally there was a series of twelve for each class. It began with the analysis of experiences of mental influences, showing how powerful mind is in its effects upon man's life, its fears, anxieties, emotional excitement, anticipations, hopes -- in general, the power of thought. Next came a discussion of the divine immanence of God in the world and in man -- the Omnipresent Wisdom , at least some small portion of which is found in every man, of however lowly a nature. Following this was a lecture on the nature of matter, in which not only were Quimby's words quoted at length and explained, but (as in the writings of Warren Felt Evans, from whom they no doubt drew) additional evidence from the great idealistic philosophies was adduced in support of Dr. Quimby's theories. Thus was provided a basis for the powerful influence of mind on mind as well as of mind on body, which they considered in great detail, drawing from their own experiences with the ill as well as the experiences of others. Much emphasis was placed on the "mental atmosphere" and the subtler phases of the mental life discovered by the healer, especially of the fact that "we are members one of another," in a very intimate sense.

The subconscious aftereffects of man's dynamic opinions were explained as leading logically to their statement of the general mental theory of disease, for which they found ample support in Dr. Quimby's manuscripts. Also there was constant reference to the teachings of the New Testament concerning disease. Man's spiritual nature was discussed at length, and here the Dressers followed Quimby in distinguishing between the historic Jesus and the Christ, "the universal ideal or consciousness," a distinction which seemed to them, as it had to Dr. Quimby and has to most New Thought leaders since, to be very important because it "made clear the possibilities open before everyone who is faithful to the guidance of the omnipresent wisdom," and served to encourage the beginner to undertake the work of spiritual healing. They were careful to insist that this in no way was to be construed as a denial of the divinity of Christ. Rather, "to the love of Christ as the elder brother was added the practical conception of the Christ ideal as the highest standard of service among the sick," something in the nature of a new revelation to many minds of the day.

In most respects it is clear that the Dressers follow closely the thought and practice of Quimby, though one gets the impression of a kind of religious warmth in them that goes beyond anything in Quimby's teachings. God is omnipresent wisdom, immanent in all the universe and man. Every man possesses in some degree God within; indeed, man has no good quality or power that is wholly his own, rather all that he possesses is God within. All the qualities of love, mercy, justice, truth that reside in man , though they are but a spark of the infinite love, or mercy, or justice, or wisdom, "yet they must be the same kind else they would not be true love, or mercy, or justice, or wisdom."

Annetta Dresser published a book in 1895 entitled *The Philosophy of P. P. Quimby* giving a historical sketch of the life and works of P. P. Quimby and outling the healing methods that he taught.

Dr. Michael H. Likey, Ph.D., D.D.

Following is the lecture given in 1887 by Julius A. Dresser.

The True History of Mental Science

The lecture was delivered at the Church of The Divine Unity, Boston, Massachusetts, Sunday, February 6th, 1887.

The following is revised with additions, and the original wording/language of the times has been retained.

Preface

The facts given in the following address have been held for many years, until there should be such a general demand for them that they would receive a willing and an unprejudiced ear, and an appreciation in accordance with their merits. Portions of this history have been contributed by this author to the "Mental Healing Monthly," of Boston, in nearly the same words as here given; and also, some portions to the "Christian Metaphysician," of Chicago. But this pamphlet includes extracts from the unpublished manuscripts of P. P. Quimby, which appear in no other publication.

The Facts Concerning The Discovery of Mental Healing

The foundation principles of what we now term Mental Science are shown by history to have been largely understood by the philosophers of all ages. The philosophy of Plato, who flourished four hundred years before Christ, was essentially one of idealism; and the same idealistic theory is found in different forms of expression set forth by leading thinkers of succeeding generations, notably by Spinoza, and by Bishop Berkeley, in the seventeenth century. But while they mainly agreed that all reality is in the realms of spirit, of which what we see is only an emanation or manifestation, they all failed to apply their views to the healing of disease. Of those who had this understanding previous to our time, only Jesus and his disciples applied it to relieving human ills; all others devoted their teachings simply to modifying and forming character.

Coming down to this nineteenth century, we find Ralph Waldo Emerson's writings tilled and permeated with the idealistic theory, and running over with the belief of an omnipresent Goodness as the substance of all things, with here and there a hint that the so-called "ills that flesh is heir to" may be eradicated as errors when held up to the light of truth, the same as can moral evils. But the first person in this age who penetrated the depths of truth so far as to discover and bring forth a true science of life, and openly apply it to the healing of the sick, was Phineas Parkhurst Quimby, of Belfast, Me. I am well aware that with some people this is a disputed point, they respecting the claims of certain others; but I have been requested, by many persons interested in this history, to say what I know about it, and, believing that the time has come to do so, I shall now give you a series of facts, and you can judge of them for yourselves.

The first that I knew of P. P. Quimby was in June, 1860, when I went to him as a patient, in Portland, Me. This was five and a half years before his death. He had then, 1860, been in the regular practice of mental healing for many years, in different towns in Maine, and had been located in Portland about two years. There was at that time, 1860, no one else in the practice in New England, nor in this country, nor in the world, so far as was then known, or has since been heard of; nor was there at that time anyone else who understood it as a science, he having been the discoverer and founder, as I think I shall show you. He had then, 1860, been at work twenty years in this field of investigation and discovery and ultimate practice, which carries his first investigations back to the year 1840.

The question may be asked, "Was Quimby ever a mesmerist?" I reply that he was, for a limited time, and for purposes of experiment and investigation. The truth came to him, not as a revelation pure and simple, but as the result of practical experiment and patient research among the phenomena of life, urged on by the impulses of an active, inquiring, comprehensive mind. I have seen extracts from newspapers as far back as 1842-3, giving accounts of his public exhibitions of mesmerism, in some of which newspaper accounts he was rated with a few others in this country and Europe who were the leading mesmerizers in the world. Dr. Quimby had been a watch and clock maker for some years, when mesmerism attracted his attention.

The subject of mesmerism was first introduced into this country by Mr. Charles Poyan, a French gentleman, in the year 1836. A few years later, a certain Dr. Collyer lectured upon it in New England and elsewhere. In 1840, P. P. Quimby commenced experimenting with it, although this did not furnish him his first lesson in the truth he afterwards developed, as I have seen from accounts of his earlier experiences. From a newspaper account of one of his public exhibitions of mesmerism in Belfast, Me., dated April 17, 1843, I make this extract: -

"Before we proceed to describe the experiments" (the newspaper says), " we will say that Mr. Quimby is a gentleman, in size rather smaller than the medium of man, with a well-proportioned and well-balanced phrenological head, and with the power of concentration surpassing anything we have ever witnessed. His eyes are black and very piercing, with rather a pleasant expression, and he possesses the power of looking at one object without even winking, for a great length of time."

In his mesmeric experiments, as reported in the Maine papers in those years so long ago, Quimby is shown to have progressed gradually *out* of mesmerism, into a knowledge of the hidden powers of mind; and he soon found in man a principle, or a power, that was not of man himself, but was higher than man, and of which he could only be a medium. Its character was goodness and intelligence; and its power was great. He also found that disease was nothing but an erroneous belief of mind. Here was a discovery of truth, and on this discovery he founded a system of treating the sick, and founded a science of life. As a better testimony than my own on these points, I will here introduce an extract from a letter I received from his son, Geo. A. Quimby, of Belfast, Me., in reply to one in which I wrote for certain data relating to his father. Speaking of his father, the son wrote as follows: -

"Some time in 1840, he became deeply interested in mesmerism, and for quite a number of years, in connection with his other business, he gave exhibitions with a clairvoyant subject through the State of Maine, and also treated disease, using his mesmeric power, as it was termed then. This method he kept up, but gradually working *out* of the mesmeric idea, into a train of reasoning of his own, which he applied to the patient, till finally he gave up putting the patient to sleep mesmerically, and followed the mode of treatment which he originated and continued up to the time of his death, which treatment, in his own words, was this: -

"He says, 'My practice is unlike all medical practice. I give no medicine, and make no outward applications. I tell the patient his troubles, and what he thinks is his disease, and my explanation is the cure. If I succeed in correcting his errors, I change the fluids of the system and establish *the truth or health. The truth is the cure.* This mode of practice applies to all cases.'"

These are Dr. Quimby's own words, and any one can see that they mean a purely mental treatment, for he speaks of what the patient thinks is his disease and calls it his error, by saying that if he succeeds in correcting the patient's errors, he then establishes the truth, and *the truth is the cure.* You see from this that he had discovered that disease was an error of mind, and nothing else, and the God-power of truth which he had discovered in man, being set up again in the victim of disease, destroyed the error or disease, and reestablished the harmony.

This discovery, you observe, was not made from the Bible, but from mental phenomena and searching investigations; and after the truth was discovered, he found his new views all portrayed and illustrated in Christ's teachings and works. If you think this seems to show that Quimby was a remarkable man, let me tell you that he was one of the most unassuming of men that ever lived, for no one could well be more so, nor make less account of his own achievements. Humility was a marked feature of his character (I knew him intimately). To this was united a benevolent and an unselfish nature, and a love of truth, with a remarkably keen perception. But the distinguishing feature of his mind was that he could not entertain an opinion, because it was not knowledge. His faculties were so practical and perceptive that the wisdom of mankind, which is largely made up of opinions, was of little use to him, hence the charge that he was not an educated man is literally true. True knowledge to him was *positive proof*, as in a problem of mathematics, therefore he discarded books and sought phenomena, where his perceptive faculties made him master of the situation. Therefore, he got from his experiments in mesmerism what other men did not get, a stepping-stone to a higher knowledge than man possessed, and a new range to mental vision. He wrote out his discoveries at great length, and from these yet unpublished writings, now in the possession of his son, before referred to, I am privileged to incorporate in this lecture the following article, which was written in the year 1863, and thus allow Quimby to tell an important part of his own story. These are his words:-

"My conversion from disease to health, and the subsequent change from belief in the medical faculty to entire disbelief in it, and to the knowledge of the truth on which I base my theory."

Can a theory be found capable of practice, which can separate truth from error? I undertake to say there is a method of reasoning, which, being understood, can separate one from the other. Men never dispute about a fact that can be demonstrated by scientific reasoning. Controversies arise from some idea that has been turned into a false direction, leading to a false position. The basis of my reasoning is this point, that whatever is true to a person, if he cannot prove it, is not necessarily true to another; therefore, because a person says a thing is no reason that he says true. The greatest evil that follows taking an opinion for a truth, is disease. Let medical and religious opinions, which produce so vast an amount of misery, be tested by the rule I have laid down, and it will be seen how much they are founded in truth. For twenty years I have been testing them, and I have failed to find one single principle of truth in either. This is not from any prejudice against the medical faculty, for when I began to investigate the mind, I was entirely on that side. I was prejudiced in favor of the medical faculty, for I never employed anyone outside of the regular faculty, nor took the least particle of quack medicine.

"Some thirty years ago I was very sick, and was considered fast wasting away with consumption. At that time I became so low that it was with difficulty I could walk about. I was all the while under the allopathy practice, and I had taken so much calomel that my system was said to be poisoned with it, and I lost many of my teeth from that effect. My symptoms were those of any consumptive, and I had been told that my liver was affected, and my kidneys were diseased, and that my lungs were nearly consumed. I believed all this, from the fact that I had all the symptoms, and could not resist the opinions of the physician while having the proof with me. In this state I was compelled to abandon my business, and losing all hope, I gave up to die. Not that I thought the medical faculty had no wisdom, but that my case was one that could not be cured.

"Having an acquaintance who cured himself by riding horseback, I thought I would try riding in a carriage, as I was too weak to ride horseback. My horse was contrary, and once, when about two miles from home, he stopped at the foot of a long hill and would not start except as I went by his side, so I was obliged to run nearly the whole distance. Having reached the top of the hill, I got into the carriage, and as I was very much exhausted, I concluded to sit there the balance of the day, if the horse did not start. Like all sickly and nervous people, I could not remain easy in that place, and seeing a man plowing, I waited till he had plowed around a three-acre lot, and got within sound of my voice, when I asked him to start my horse. He did so, and at the time, I was so weak I could scarcely lift my whip. But excitement took possession of my senses, and I drove the horse as fast as I could go, up hill and down, till I reached home, and when I got into the stable I felt as strong as I ever did." (The account of this experience ends here, but it seems to have been a phenomenon that opened Quimby's eyes, and through his keen perceptions it taught him a great deal. The article continues with an experience of another nature. J. A. D.)

"When I commenced to mesmerize, I was not well, according to the medical science, but in my researches I found a remedy for my disease. Here was where I first discovered that mind was matter, and capable of being changed.

"Also, that disease being a deranged state of mind, the cause I found to exist in our belief. The evidence of this theory I found in myself, for like all others I had believed in medicine. Disease and its power over life, and its curability, are all embraced in our belief. Some believe in various remedies, and others believe that the spirits of the dead prescribe. I have no confidence in the virtue of either. I know that cures have been made in these ways. I do not deny them. But the principle on which they are done is the question to solve, for disease can be cured, with or without medicine, on *but one principle*. I have said I believed in the old practice, and its medicines, the effect of which I had within myself; for, knowing no other way to account for the phenomena, I took it for granted that they were the result of medicine.

"With this mass of evidence staring me in the face, how could I doubt the old practice? Yet, in spite of all my prejudices, I had to yield to a stronger evidence than man's opinion, and discard the whole theory of medicine, practiced by a class of men, some honest, some ignorant, some selfish, and all thinking that the world must be ruled by their opinions.

"Now for my particular experience. I had pains in the back, which they said were caused by my kidneys, which were partially consumed. I also was told that I had ulcers on my lungs. Under this belief, I was miserable enough to be of no account in the world. This was the state I was in when I commenced to mesmerize. On one occasion, when I had my subject asleep, he described the pains I felt in my back (I had never dared to ask him to examine me, for I felt sure that my kidneys were nearly gone), and he placed his hand on the spot where I felt the pain. He then told me that my kidneys were in a very bad state; that one was half consumed, and a piece three inches long had separated from it, and was only connected by a slender thread. This was what I believed to be true, for it agreed with what the doctors told me, and with what I had suffered, for I had not been free from pain for years. My common-sense told me that no medicine would ever cure this trouble, and therefore I must suffer till death relieved me. But I asked him if there was any remedy? He replied, ' Yes, I can put the piece on so it will grow, and you will get well.' At this, I was completely astonished, and knew not what to think. He immediately placed his hands upon me, and said he united the pieces so they would grow. The next day he said they had grown together, and from that day I never have experienced the least pain from them.

"Now what is the secret of the cure? I had not the least doubt but that I was as he described ; and if he had said, its I expected that he would, that nothing could be done, I should have died in a year or so. But when he said he could cure me in the way he proposed, I began to think, and I discovered that I had been deceived into a belief that made me sick. The absurdity of his remedies made me doubt the fact that my kidneys were diseased, for he said in two days they were as well as ever. If he saw the first condition, he also saw the last, for in both cases he said he could see. I concluded in the first instance that he read my thoughts, and when he said he could cure me, he drew on his own mind; and his ideas were so absurd that the disease vanished by the absurdity of the cure. This was the first stumbling-block I found in the medical science. I soon ventured to let him examine me further, and in every case he would describe my feelings, but would vary about the amount of disease, and his explanation and remedies always convinced me that I had no such disease, and that my troubles were of my own make.

"At this time I frequently visited the sick with Lucius, by invitation of the attending physician, and the boy examined the patient, and told facts that would astonish everybody, and yet every one of them were believed. For instance, he told a person affected as I had been, only worse, that his lungs looked like a honeycomb, and his liver was covered with ulcers. He then prescribed some simple herb tea and the patient recovered, and the doctor believed the medicine cured him. But I believed that the doctor made the disease, and his faith in the boy made a change in the mind, and the cure followed. Instead of gaining confidence in the doctors, I was forced to the conclusion that their science is false. Man is made up of truth and belief, and if he is deceived into a belief that he has, or is liable to have a disease, the belief is catching and the effect follows it. I have given the experience of my emancipation from this belief and from confidence in the doctors, so that it may open the eyes of those who stand where I was. I have risen from this belief, and I return to warn my brethren, lest when they are disturbed they shall get into this place of torment prepared by the medical faculty. Having suffered myself, I cannot take advantage of my fellow-men by introducing a new mode of curing disease and prescribing medicine. My theory exposes the hypocrisy of those who undertake to cure in that way. They make ten diseases to one cure, thus bringing a surplus of misery into the world, and shutting out a healthy state of society. They have a monopoly, and no theory that lessens disease can compete with them. When I cure there is one disease the less ; but not so when others cure, for the supply of sickness shows that there is more disease on hand than there ever was. Therefore, the labor for health is slow, and the manufactory of disease is greater. The newspapers teem with advertisements of remedies, showing that the supply of disease increases. My theory teaches man to manufacture health, and when people go into this occupation, disease will diminish, and those who furnish disease and death will be few and scarce."

This account from Dr, Quimby himself, settles many things. First, it gives in detail *one* of the *many* experiences by which he discovered this truth. It shows, also, the practical nature of the man's mind, and illustrates his wonderful perceptive powers. And the article shows that no one could have written it but himself; and it shows, too, that what he arrived at was the knowledge that disease is nothing but an error of belief, to be corrected by the truth. On this basis he practiced ever afterwards. How could he do otherwise, after making such a discovery? And this discovery was made about forty-five years ago, All these facts can be fully substantiated by consulting certain back newspaper files, and certain other persons who are familiar with it all. And this theory, that disease is an error of belief to be corrected by the truth, not only formed the basis of a science of health which Dr. Quimby introduced, but in various delineations it is the subject of voluminous manuscripts which he wrote, besides copious other writings upon a true science of life and happiness ; and others in which he explained and defended Christ's sayings, his gospel and his work. He also wrote upon the true standard of law, and of government, and upon other topics. All these writings I have read, being in the confidence of Mr. Geo. A. Quimby, the son, who holds them; and I can testify that no such depth of understanding has yet seen the light, in print, as those manuscripts contain. This son was with his father as secretary, during the father's last five years of practice, and the father hoped that his son would take up the practice with him, and succeed him, but he took a different turn, and is a manufacturer.

I think I can see a wisdom in nearly everything. If those writings had been published, as Dr. Quimby intended, in his day, or even at any time since, previous to now, they would have found a public unprepared for them. Therefore they are in the hands of a person whose sympathies are not stirred by a work in the truth, as some of ours are to issue them before their time. But those manuscripts will be published at a future day. The present owner of them is not troubled in the least, nor am I, that such misstatements, to call them by no worse name, as have appeared in certain printed publications, belying and belittling Dr. Quimby and your speaker; nor by the efforts to show that Dr. Quimby's manuscripts were written by somebody else. We have only pity for a person who would make such misstatements, for a purely selfish purpose. You have heard or read of Haman's gallows, which he built for Mordecai, the Jew, and how they finally hung only the builder himself! P. P. Quimby's writings when published will speak for themselves, and his friends know it perfectly. They pay no attention to what is said or done by others, any more than your speaker does.

One more point of a personal nature, and I pass on to more general facts. I have been blamed many times by persons for so long withholding the facts I now make public, together with much more that I shall not mention at this time. The reply that myself and wife have always made was, that we wished to pursue our work in the truth in the true spirit of that truth, which is charity and love, and this did not lead us to say aught against another, nor even to reply to unjust aspersions upon ourselves or P. P. Quimby. We knew that some time the facts would be called for by supporters of the truth, and then, if we felt the time had come, we would give them, and in so doing, the relation of the facts would be seen plainly to be done only for the truth's sake, and in its true spirit.

But, said some, people are being deceived constantly. We replied that we knew it, but that very many things were allowed by an overruling Providence to go on in this world which seemed to need correction, and we were not running this world nor the universe, and we were more particular to see that we discharged our own immediate duties and what little good we might do, to the best of our ability, and in the spirit of love, than we were to follow the prevailing human custom of taking upon ourselves the assumed work of correcting errors that other people were falling into. I acknowledge that our course has been open to criticism on this one point; but, dear friends, we have waited "with malice toward none and charity for all" for your call for these facts, and now we can give them because they are wanted, and not because of any pleasure it might be said we had in doing it, for that phase of this relation which constitutes unavoidable reflection upon others is only painful, and I have avoided it as much as possible in giving this account, and have therefore left out a *great deal* of detail that might otherwise have been included, and have made no replies at all to the many unjust and *false* statements that have been published and circulated about P. P. Quimby and myself. No one has been really injured as a result of our reticence, I trust, and certainly we have not suffered in any respect, except one, and that is that persons have said, and others have thought, that because we made no replies to anything, that there were none that we could make, and therefore all claims and statements of others were true. Do you remember the words of the apostle: "Charity suffereth long, and is kind ; is not easily provoked, thinketh no evil, rejoiceth not in iniquity, but rejoiceth in the truth; charity never faileth "?

Such is the spirit of the kind of truth that I learned from P. P. Quimby, and the kind that he himself practiced. And his spirit of love so opened his soul to the God-power that his works were marvellous. The quick cures that he brought about have not been equalled by anyone else since his time, that I know of. Myself and wife have owed our lives to him for nearly twenty-seven years past, and to the truth he revealed to us. Thousands of others could make a similar testimony; but I prefer not to occupy time with relating his cures. The man himself never desired publicity; the truth itself and the good of humanity were the first and last considerations with him. He even had no fixed name for his theory or practice, desiring to be known only by his fruits. He sank the individual wholly in the cause of truth and the good of humanity.

It is the intention of your speaker to so relate this history as to avoid any appearance of fulsome praise, because the man Quimby would not desire it, and it is my aim only to relate plain facts in a plain manner, and I request you therefore to consider no statement herein as overdrawn. Your attention is called to one important fact, and that is, that the kind of individual I am describing in the person of P. P. Quimby, is the kind who *can make discoveries of truth*, if any one can ; that is, a mind of great capabilities, coupled with great humility and extreme unselfishness. This is the kind of a medium that God speaks through, because such a soul is open to his inspirations. On the other hand, a selfish soul, who seeks personal aggrandizement, is not open to revelations of much moment, because selfishness always blinds one, the truth does not flourish in such a soil.

P. P. Quimby's perceptive powers were something remarkable. He always told the patient, at the first sitting, what the latter thought was his disease; and as he was able to do this, he never allowed the patient to tell him anything about his case. Quimby would also continue and tell to the patient what the circumstances were which first caused the trouble, and then explain to him how he fell into his error, and then from this basis prove to him, in many instances, that his state of suffering was purely an error of mind, and not what he thought it was. Thus his system of treating diseases was really and truly a science, which proved itself. You see, also, from these statements, how he taught his patients to understand, and how persons who went to him for treatment were instructed in the truth, as well as restored to health. In this way some persons became especially instructed, as did your speaker. The persons referred to also obtained many private interviews with him, for further instruction in the truth.

The question has often been asked, by persons who had gotten some idea of the truth, how Dr, Quimby, who was a man of such power and understanding, came to die? Herein lies a story of his unselfishness. The man was overrun with patients for many years, and he was alone in the work. There is always a limit to finite endurance, and his heart was too large to enable him to refuse people whom he might help out of their sufferings when they applied to him. During those years when his office was in Portland, his home and family being always in Belfast, he was compelled once in four or six weeks to get away from the pressing tide of humanity, and go home to Belfast, privately, and rest for three or four days.

He sometimes would say to those nearest him, that if he ever should allow himself to get so far exhausted as not to be able to recover himself, there was no one to help him, and he would be compelled to go out. But, though he never expected to overdo to that extent, it is just what happened. In brief, he laid down his life for the sick, and died in their cause at the age of sixty-five years, twenty-one years ago.

Nearly all in those days, who were willing to try a practitioner outside of the medical schools, were persons who had exhausted every means of help within those schools, and when finally booked for the grave, they would send for or go to Quimby. As he expressed it, they would send for him and the undertaker at the same time, and the one who got there first would get the case. Consequently, his battle with error, alone and single-handed, was a hard one, especially as in those days there was much less liberality than now.

Some may desire to ask if, in his practice, he ever in any way used manipulation? I reply that, in treating a patient, after he had finished his explanations, and the silent work, *which completed the treatment*, he usually rubbed the head two or three minutes, in a brisk manner, for the purpose of letting the patient see that something was done. This was a measure of securing the confidence of the patient, at a time when he was starting a new practice, and stood alone in it. I knew him to make many and quick cures at a distance sometimes with persons he never saw at all. He never considered the touch of the hand as at all necessary, but let it be governed by circumstances, as was done 1800 years ago.

But, dear friends, I do not wish you to rely upon my statements alone for the facts of this history, and of this man's character, his discoveries, and his works. To what has already been given from the words of others, still further testimonies may be added. That able writer upon Mental Science, Dr. W. F. Evans, pays the following tribute to Quimby, is his second volume, entitled " Mental Medicine." He says: "Disease being in its root a *wrong belief*, change that belief, and we cure the disease . . . The late Dr. Quimby, of Portland, one of the most successful healers of this or any age, embraced this view of the nature of disease, and by a long succession of most remarkable cures . . . . proved the truth of the theory. . . . . Had he lived in a remote age or country, the wonderful facts which occurred in his practice would have now been deemed either mythical or miraculous. He seemed to reproduce the wonders of the gospel history," Dr. Evans obtained this knowledge of Quimby mainly when he visited him as a patient, making two visits for that purpose, about the year 1863, an interesting account of which I received from him, at East Salisbury, in the year 1876. Dr. Evans had been a clergyman up to the year 1863, and was then located in Claremont, N. H. But so readily did he understand the explanations of Quimby, which his Swedenborgian faith enabled him to grasp the more quickly, that he told Quimby at the second interview that he thought he could himself cure the sick in this way. Quimby replied that he thought he could. His first attempts on returning home were so successful that the preacher became a practitioner from that time, and the result has been great growth in the truth and the accomplishment of a great and a good work during the nearly twenty-five years since then. Dr. Evans's six volumes upon the subject of Mental Healing have had a wide and a well-deserved sale.

Amongst those who were friends as well as patients of Quimby during the years from 1860 to 1865, and who paid high tributes to his discoveries of truth, and the consequent good to many people and to the world, was one who, for some strange reason, afterwards changed and followed a different course, with which you all are more or less familiar. I refer to the author of the book "Science and Health". As she had, during several years, special opportunities to know the man and to learn truth of him, this record would he incomplete without including her testimony at that time. Fortunately, it can be given in her own words and you can form your own estimate of them. The proof that they are her own words, and also that the statements of this lecture are correct, may be obtained by addressing Mr. Geo. A. Quimby, of Belfast, Me., and also other persons whose names I will furnish on application.

When the lady became a patient of Quimby she at once took an interest in his theory, and imbibed his explanations of truth rapidly. She also took a bold stand, and published an account of her progress in health in a daily paper. The following is an extract from her first article thus published, which appeared in the Portland *Evening Courier* in June, 1862 :-

"When our Shakespeare decided that ' there were more things in this world than were dreamed of in your philosophy,' I cannot say of a verity that he had a foreknowledge of P. P. Quimby. And when the school Platonic anatomized the soul and divided it into halves, to be reunited by elementary attractions, and heathen philosophers averred that old Chaos in sullen silence brooded o'er the earth until her inimitable form was hatched from the egg of night, I would not at present decide whether the fallacy was found in their premises or conclusions, never having dated my existence before the flood. When the startled alchemist discovered, as he supposed, an universal solvent, or the philosopher's stone, and the more daring Archimedes invented a lever wherewithal to pry up the universe, I cannot say that in either the principle obtained in nature or in art, or that it worked well, having never tried it. But when by a falling apple an immutable law was discovered, we gave it the crown of science, which is incontrovertible and capable of demonstration; hence, that was wisdom and truth. When from the evidence of the senses my reason takes cognizance of truth, although it may appear in quite a miraculous view, I must acknowledge that as science, which is truth uninvestigated. Hence the following demonstration:-

"Three weeks since, I quitted my nurse and sick-room *en route* for Portland. The belief of my recovery had died out of the hearts of those who were most anxious for it. With this mental and physical depression I first visited P. P. Quimby, and in less than one week from that time I ascended by a stairway of one hundred and eighty-two steps to the dome of the City Hall, and am improving *ad infinitum*. To the most subtle reasoning, such a proof, coupled, too, as it is with numberless similar ones, demonstrates his power to heal.

Now for a brief analysis of this power.

"Is it Spiritualism? Listen to the words of wisdom. 'Believe in God, believe also in me ; or believe me for the very work's sake.' Now, then, his works are but the result of superior wisdom which can demonstrate a science not understood; hence, it were a doubtful proceeding not to believe him for the work's sake. Well, then, he denies that his power to heal the sick is borrowed from the spirits of this or another world ; and let us take the Scriptures for proof. 'A kingdom divided against itself cannot stand. 'How, then, can he receive the friendly aid of the disenthralled spirit, while he rejects the faith of the solemn mystic who crosses the threshold of the dark unknown to conjure up from the vasty deep the awestruck spirit of some invisible squaw?

"Again, is it by animal magnetism that he heals the sick?

Let us examine. I have employed electro-magnetism and animal magnetism, and for a brief interval have felt relief from the equilibrium which I fancied was restored to an exhausted system, or by a diffusion of concentrated action; but in no instance did I get rid of a return of all my ailments, because I had not been helped out of the error in which opinion involved us. My operator believed in disease independent of the mind; hence, I could not be wiser than my teacher. But now I can see dimly at first, and only as trees walking the great principle which underlies Dr. Quimby's faith and works; and just in proportion to my right perception of truth is my recovery. This truth which he opposes to the error of giving intelligence to matter and placing pain where it never placed itself, if received understandingly, changes the currents of the system to their normal action, and the mechanism of the body goes on undisturbed. That this is a science capable of demonstration becomes clear to the minds of those patients who reason upon the process of their cure. The truth which he establishes in the patient cures him (although he may be wholly unconscious thereof), and the body which is full of light, is no longer in disease. At present, I am too much in error to elucidate the truth, and can touch only the key-note for the master hand to wake the harmony. May it be in essays instead of notes, say I. After all, this is a very spiritual doctrine; but the eternal years of God are with it, and it must stand firm as the rock of ages. And to many a poor sufferer may it be found, as by me, ' the shadow of a great rock in a weary land.'"

It will be observed by noting the foregoing statements closely, that the lady did not understand that disease is a state of mind and the truth is its cure, until this experience with Quimby took place; and it will be seen how rapidly, during the three weeks' experience referred to, she had been taking in that truth, and seeing that it was a true science, and that it was curing herself. It is now easy to see just *when* and just *where* she "discovered Christian science."

The day following the publication of her article, it was criticised by the Portland *Advertiser*, and she then wrote a second article, replying to the criticism, In it appeared the following paragraph, referring to Quimby and his doctrine:-

"P. P. Quimby stands upon the plane of wisdom with his truth. Christ healed the sick, but not by jugglery or with drugs ; as the former speaks as never man before spake, and heals as never man healed since Christ, is he not identified with truth, and is not this the Christ which is in him? We know that in wisdom is life, `and the life was the light of man, 'P. P. Quimby rolls away the stone from the sepulchre of error, and health is the resurrection. But we also know that 'light shineth in darkness, and the darkness comprehended it not.'"

These extracts are in plain language and they speak for themselves. The statements are made with too evident an understanding of their truth to be doubted or questioned, or afterwards reversed in any particular. It should be borne in mind that your speaker was there at the time and was familiar with all the circumstances she relates, and the views expressed. The devoted regard the lady formed for her deliverer, Quimby, and for the truth he taught her, which proved her salvation, was continued to be held by her from this time (the summer of 1862) up to a period at least four years later; for in January, 1866, Quimby's death occurred, and on Feb. 15 she sent to me a copy of a poem she had written to his memory, and accompanied it by a letter commencing in these words: "I inclose some lines of mine, in memory of our much-loved friend, which, perhaps, you will not think overwrought in meaning; others must, of course."

The poem, which had been printed in a Lynn newspaper, is as follows:-

Lines On the Death of Dr. P.P. Quimby, Who Healed With the Truth that Christ Taught, in Contradiction to all Isms:
Did sackcloth clothe the sun, and day grow night
All matter mourn the hour with dewy eyes,
When Truth, receding from our mortal sight,
Had paid to error her last sacrifice?
Can we forget the power that gave us life?
Shall we forget the wisdom of its way?
Then ask me not, amid this mortal strife-
This keenest pang of animated clay-
To mourn him less; to mourn him more, were just,
If to his memory 't were a tribute given
For solemn, sacred, earnest trust
Delivered to us ere he rose to heaven
"Heaven but the happiness of that calm soul,
Growing in stature to the throne of God;
Rest should reward him who hath made us whole,
Seeking, though tremblers, where his footsteps trod."

Oh, that in an evil hour she had never been tempted to erase the sentiments of that poem, which was *not* an overwrought tribute to the memory of our much-loved friend!

But let that charity which rejoiceth not in iniquity, but rejoiceth in the truth, and never faileth, not fail even here; for we have the truth to rejoice in; this truth which P. P. Quimby brought forth, and for years labored so unceasingly to give it to the world, and finally laid down his life in its cause, - this glorious truth is still blessing us, and it will do so more and more unto the perfect day. It is a revelation of truth that makes us free indeed! And we have only to set aside self-love and self-glory and work earnestly in this cause, by every word and deed of love that opportunity offers, to find ourselves growing gradually into all wisdom and understanding, and out of and away from every ill and every form of unhappiness in existence.

I cannot better close this address than by quoting an extract from one of P. P. Quimby's manuscripts, which will show the spirit of the man, as well as give an indication of the truth he preached : -

"Every disease is the invention of man, and has no identity in wisdom; but to those who believe it, it is a truth. If everything man does not understand were blotted out, what is there left, of man? Would he be better, or worse, if nine tenths of all he thinks he knows were blotted out of his mind, and he existed with what is true?

"I contend that he would, as it were, sit on the clouds and see the world beneath him tormented with ideas that form living errors, whose weight is ignorance. Safe from their power he would not return to the world's belief for any consideration.

"In a slight degree, this is my case. I sit as it were in another world or condition, as far above the belief in disease as the heavens are above the earth, and though safe myself, I grieve for the sins of my fellow-man; and I am reminded of the words of Jesus when he beheld the misery of his countrymen: 'O Jerusalem'. How oft would I have gathered thee as a hen gathereth her chickens, but ye would not.'

"I hear this truth now pleading with man, to listen to the voice of reason. I know from my own experience with the sick that their troubles are the effect of their own belief; not that their belief is the truth, but their beliefs act upon their minds, bringing them into subjection to their belief, and their troubles are a change that follows.

"Disease is a reality to all mankind; but I do not include myself, because I stand outside of it, where I can see things real to the world and things that are real to wisdom. I know that I can distinguish that which is false from a truth, in religion, or in disease. To me, disease is always false; but to those who believe it, it is a truth, and the errors in religion the same. Until the world is shaken by investigation, so that the rocks and mountains of religious error are removed, and the medical Babylon destroyed, sickness and sorrow will prevail. Feeling as I do, and seeing so many young people go the broad road to destruction, I can say from the bottom of my soul: O Priestcraft! Fill up the measure of your cups of iniquity, for on your head will come, sooner or later, the sneers and taunts of the people. Your theory will be overthrown by the voice of wisdom, that will rouse the men of science, who will battle your error, and drive you utterly from the face of the earth. Then there will arise a new science, followed by a new mode of reasoning, which shall teach man that to be wise and well is to unlearn his errors."

▼

CHAPTER 3

Mind-Treatments In-Depth: A Clinic

The Intake

Your patient is sitting before you in your office. You've taken the basic information such as name, address, phone numbers. They have expressed to you what unwanted behavior, feelings, emotions, and/or thoughts they wish to eliminate.

Using the previous systems of personality analysis you have them categorized, so you know the best wording to use; you know what anchor is best for them: God, Source, Love, Light…whichever fits into their belief-system. You even know which traumas need healing. You are ready to proceed with the actual Mind-Treatment.

The Mind-Treatment

You must now at this point induce self-hypnosis, or a mild meditative state.

As outlined previously, I prefer sitting eye-to-eye with my clients, as opposed to the traditional "therapist's" approach of them reclining on a sofa;

they tend to feel too vulnerable and out of control lying down. I highly recommend you use any of the fine induction scripts available in William Hewitt's book "Hypnosis for Beginners"; even after I had graduated from Robert Shield's excellent College of Hypnotherapy with a diploma in Clinical Hypnotherapy, I preferred using Mr. Hewitt's scripts, which I still do to this day. They are excellent for weight control, stop smoking, past life regressions, and more. Use them; he recommends (as do I) that you copy the wording down on handy index-cards until you know the words by heart. Needless to say, the inductions and deepenings are invaluable. Inductions involve having the patient focusing on something, and relax; they may do this by listening to either a repetitive auditory focal point (sound of a clock, your voice), a visual focal-point (candle-flame, hypnotic wheel, swinging pendulum/pocket-watch) or physical relaxation (light-touch massage). It's been long-known that if the subject/client/patient strains slightly their eyes up and back, the eyes will tire and gradually close, "feeling heavy". You can achieve this by holding an object just above their head and back, and having them fixate on it while you verbally lull them into an altered-state. I used to have a dot on the ceiling of my office for them to stare at while they were lying down; of course the position of the dot forced them to look up and back. A mystical-meditation method is to have the subject close their eyes, and with lids shut, look up and back into their head at their mythological "third eye", located at the forehead area. Science has proven that doing this for approximately one minute causes the brain to enter into alpha (or mild-meditative) state.

I recommend that you also have your patient take a few deep, full breaths, and then exhale; this creates an automatic physiological response that relaxes them. Other Induction techniques include a tightening of individual muscles and relaxing of them, for example tightening and releasing stomach-muscles, arm-muscles, buttocks, leg-muscles, etc. one at a time. Pick any one of these and use them.

Then you must perform any one of numerous "deepenings", to insure that they go into a receptive, altered-state.

My favorite deepening is giving them the visualization of them walking down 10 steps from a long, winding staircase, one-step-at a time, until they reach the floor below; I get them to "feel" the smooth, polished wood of the handrail, and the soft carpeting beneath their feet. The sensual feelings help them to go under, as it makes the experience of the visualization more real to them. Other deepenings include the visualization of them going down 10 floors in an elevator, with them watching the numbers going down, and going down on an escalator, to name just a few. The idea is that they are "relaxing more and more" as they go down lower and lower. I'll often use Hewitt's deepening visualizations of them seeing their name written in the sky by a sky-writing airplane, focusing on the alphabet being said slowly backwards, and a sandbag heavily resting on their legs, filled with an anesthetic that slowly sinks into their body.

Whatever you use, they must slowly and willingly sink into a deep altered-state; most people feel comfortable with you referring to this state as a "meditative" state, as opposed to "hypnotic" state, which has mind-manipulative connotations.

Quimby sat face-to-face with his patients, as do I; again, they feel less vulnerable than if they were lying down. He then proceeded to "talk" them into an altered-state by having them stare into his eyes as a fixation-point (I do the same), sometimes holding their hands so that they feel secure; I will sometimes do this too, if it is appropriate, and within the comfort-zone of my patient. I also place a small pillow on our knees, so that there is a psychological "distance" between us. This pillow also makes a great "working-surface" for them to place their hands on, if they don't want me to hold or touch their hands. I too "talk them" into an altered-state.

"Talking" Them into Altered-State

I don't recommend this method if you're new to hypnosis. You might not know what to say, or falter. Have them close their eyes and read from induction and deepening scripts.

Because I have years of experience, they feel my confidence, which also puts them at ease. I don't use standard induction and deepening verbage anymore as previously described for the mind-treatments, only for the Clinical Hypnotherapy sessions; I use my eyes as a fixation-point for my patients, also having them focusing on their breathing as I speak. I have them think "one" on their inhalation and "two" on their exhalation. I condition them at this point to verbally respond to my questions while focusing in on my eyes and the "one-two, one-two" by asking them questions that they can respond "yes" or "no" to. This accomplishes several things: it distracts them from the process, thus making them go deeper, and gives them a false sense of control, since they can "consciously" answer my questions.

I ask them things based on the information gathered in the intake; questions that are positive and affirming, such as "Do you believe in God/a Higher-Power?" (if I uncovered in the intake that they do, of course) This reinforces their belief and puts them even more at ease. Other questions such as "…and you're feeling great, aren't you?" and "…you want to heal completely, don't you?" are very powerful as well.

Then, I throw in an additional command/suggestion: as they're answering me, focusing on my eyes and their breath-counting, I have them start to see a light in their heart, "getting brighter and warmer, feeling loving and secure." This suggests "God" and "God's protection" subtly to them. I get them to describe the color(s) of this light as well. We will eventually use this light to heal whatever ails them, as I reinforce the feelings of love, protection, gratitude associated with this light, and the healing, transformative properties of this light too. I even get them to see themselves surround those who have previously hurt them with this light, thus "blessing" or "forgiving" those people, after all, I reinforce, "they need the healing and blessings more than you do."

To recap, during the induction-process of "talking" them into an altered-state, I get them to mentally multi-task: mentally counting one/two, one/two while focusing on their breathing, focusing in on my eyes continually while I ask them positive, reinforcing questions culled from the intake (often, like Quimby, I'll allow my intuition to guide my questions/statements here), and finally having them "see"/visualize "God's Light" growing brighter and stronger, warmer and more loving" from the centre of their heart, describing the color(s) of this light too.

The Journey

It is at this point in the Mind-Treatment that we go on a "journey" to the time(s) that their trauma(s) occurred. I reassure them that they will feel nothing, that emotionally it will be easy, because they are "protected inside and out with God's love and strength", and because they will also "see everything like a movie on a screen, with no emotions, only actions and occurrences". Staring into each others' eyes, I reinforce with "You understand this, right? Still focusing on the one/two, one/two and your Light."

I get them to see themselves as they are now, visiting the time/place of the trauma(s), one trauma at a time, strong now with "God's love and protection". I get them to help/support their old/past self, as the trauma/incident occurs, filling the younger them with light, love, healing, and protection. They then fill the ones that hurt them with this same light and love, blessing and forgiving them finally releasing the incident(s). A group hug occurs, with a final surrounding inside and out of God's light. I ask the patient to describe the feelings they have now, reinforcing the permanence of the healing that just took place.

This all takes about 30-minutes, depending on how many past traumas we must go to. I also reinforce that whenever the patient wants to feel loved, healed and protected, all they need do is take a deep breath and exhale, focus on the one/two, one/two, and see God's light within and around them.

I teach the details of the Mind Treatment in weekend seminars. If you're interested, you can contact me here: dr.michaellikey@gmail.com

The De-Briefing

At this point, I bring my patient back to their "physical, outside world once again", by counting mentally with me up, from five up to one: "Five, you're becoming aware of your physical body, four, you can feel your toes, hands, and body, three, you're looking forward to being completely aware of your physical surroundings, two, and one, completely awake, feeling great", or words to that effect. Remember to use those great hypnotic scripts from Hewitt. I then reinforce everything, and the success of the session, with the previously-mentioned muscle-testing. I ask my patient to resist as hard as they can my trying to break their looped fingers while they say a truth (their name, age, sex); they have great strength when they do this. I then ask them to tell me a lie, and of course, they have no strength: I can break the finger-loop! I get them to say they "are whole, healed, and complete"; they do, and they are strong and won't let me separate their second-finger and thumb; finally, I get them to say the positive feelings, strengths, and emotions reinforced in the session, and again, they see that it worked: they won't let me break the loop. This proves to both of us that the session worked, and any past negative thoughts, feelings and emotions have been replaced with positive, self-empowered ones. They are truly free, their soul is healed, and they are spiritually liberated.

PART 4-

MIND-TREATMENTS AND OTHER SIMILAR THERAPIES

▼

CHAPTER I

Clinical Hypnotherapy

As previously outlined, the similarities between Clinical Hypnotherapy and meditative Mind-Treatments are numerous.

Both are used to heal the mind on an unconscious-level of traumas, thus eliminating conscious fears and self-sabotaging behaviors. Mind Treatments, therefore, like Self-Hypnosis, it may be used to eliminate the root-causes of over-eating, and other self-destructive behaviors rooted in self-loathing and low self-esteem. With both Self-Hypnosis and the Mind-Treatments, the brainwaves are either "Alpha" (light meditative state) or "Theta" (near sleep).

Like past-life regression used in hypnotherapy, Mind Treatments take the patient backward in time, facing those situations that previously caused their fears and low self-esteem.

Like hypnotherapy and NLP (Neuro Linguistic Programming), a healthier "anchor", or belief, visual, feeling/emotion is substituted for the unhealthy emotion/thought/visual/incident.

The main difference, however, between hypnosis and the Mind Treatments is the spiritual aspect.

Spiritual Aspect

With the Mind Treatments, the patient forgives/blesses, substitutes anger/resentment/fear that they formerly held towards whomever hurt them, for love, understanding, compassion, and in many cases gratitude and appreciation for the person and actions that caused their hurt. Thus, closure and healing is achieved on an emotional and spiritual level for the patient.

This anchor, if you will, of forgiveness and appreciation has been proven (in my years of study) to be permanent, and therefore longer lasting than merely substituting fear and shock, sadness and "victim-mentality" for happiness, and self-empowerment through a shifting of perceptions of the incidents. Rather, self-empowerment is achieved through the anchoring of an easily-accessible and ever-growing, omnipresent, omnipotent God/Source/Light that the patient may simply "breathe into" (I condition them to take a deep breath of "sacred-breath" whenever they feel anything less than happy, strong and empowered, in addition to visualizing the "God-Light" that they saw during the treatment).

This spiritual aspect is what makes the Mind-Treatments unique to other modalities. Rather than a mere shift of perceptions of the traumatic people and incidents, a more permanent, accessible "power" is planted in the mind of the patient. A power that they can access 24/7; like the "sponsors" of Alcoholics Anonymous, the patient can "call on" their omnipotent "sponsor" anytime, anyplace if they falter.

Other Similar Therapies/Modalities

Direct comparisons may be drawn between my Mind Treatments and the spiritual/metaphysical healing practices of Unity Church, Religious Science, and Christian Science, as they all more or less evolved out of P.P. Quimby's Mind Treatments.

In fact, part of the curriculum of my alma maters, the University of Metaphysics and the University of Sedona, was (and still is) the study and practice of such Meditative Mind Treatments, also referred to as "Metaphysical/Spiritual Healing". One of the major differences between these treatments and my Mind-Treatments, is emphasis on God as a healer of the general causes behind the illnesses, versus our slightly more clinical approach to healing the specific root-causes of the problem. With the Spiritual/Metaphysical healings, there is no probing to discover the root-causes, nor is there the proof of healing at the end, using the muscle-testing.

The process generally is: sitting in quiet contemplation, either with the patient present, or in the case of "Absent-Healing" (another difference between our Mind Treatments and Spiritual Healing is that the patient is always present), the patient expecting at a predetermined time, the treatment. The Metaphysician then focuses on making Divine-contact within themselves, then Divine-contact within the patient's mind. Once this "link" has been established through visualization, the Metaphysician calls on God for the healing of the specific person by uttering their name, and affirming that the healing has started. After a few moments of focusing on the healing of the patient (either generally, or specifically if the ailment is known), then the Metaphysician affirms and declares verbally or mentally that the patient is now "whole, healed, and complete, mind, body, and soul", acknowledges the healing that occurred, "letting it be so", and then closing with "and so it is!" to add further permanence to it.

With the currently-popular "Theta Healing", both the therapist and the patient sit face-to-face, also with a pillow on their knees. Probing questions are asked to determine the unwanted thoughts, emotions, and behaviors that the client wants to have healed, then the therapist proceeds to introduce muscle-testing to establish the effectiveness of it, stating that it will be used at the end of the treatment (as we do) to prove the effectiveness/success of the therapy. Both sit silently for the duration of the treatment, often with eyes shut, and Divine-contact established, much as in the Metaphysical Healings. Source is then asked to heal the root-causes contained within the mind of the patient, and more empowering words, concepts, phrases substituted within the mind of the client for the former thoughts, etc. Source is then asked to seal everything, as the client then experiences the muscle-testing, as in my Mind-Treatments at the end of the session.

Similarities between clinical hypnotherapy, Theta-Healing, Spiritual/Metaphysical Healing, and my Mind-Treatments are now somewhat obvious, as are the differences.

CHAPTER 2

▼

Physical Health

Dis-Ease

As previously discussed, we are all "Psycho-Physical Units", that is to say, the mind affects the body and the body affects the mind. If we are not emotionally feeling well, it is always reflected in our physical body, be it in our posture, or actual physical unwellness, or "dis-ease". We are not "at ease" (or happy), therefore our body's immune-system becomes compromised due to an upset of the chemistry and physiology of our body, and we begin to become physically unwell. Conversely, if we feel physically unwell, our moods and emotions are less than happy.

The key to all of this is healing the soul.

If the root-causes, contained within the soul (accessed through the mind) are healed, then the mind, and then the body are healed. Heal the soul, heal the mind, and heal the body.

Change your Mind, Change your Life

Simply put, "change your mind, and you change your life". We have explained how the mind works; how at the very centre and nucleus of the mind (and all things) is Source: Eternal wellness and prosperity. This is the very power that has healed and maintained us, time and time again. This is the very same power that heals a cut on our hands, even if we do nothing. The regenerative-process is Source itself! Source is always expanding, becoming better and better, growing and growing. We are the individualized expression of Source: we look like humans, but are actually God at the centre of ourselves, working Its way up and out through us, doing only the Highest good; this is why we have come into this life: to allow the Highest good to work through ourselves; some say we are here to do "service"; this is only one example of Highest good. We cannot stop the process of something greater than ourselves working through us…at least not for too long.

This is why you are reading this; either to add more knowledge to your life so that you can lead a happier, more prosperous life, another form of Highest good; being happy and prosperous, perhaps even sharing it, is also doing/living Highest good.

Allowing through the process of the Mind-Treatments, Source to work its way up from the centre of our mind and therefore our soul, healing the causes of ill emotional health there, will also result in the healing of our physical body in the process. Healing the soul, results in the healing of the mind, and the healing of the body. All are one, holistic system, intertwined. Healing of the body results in our emotionally feeling better, therefore our emotional-state (mind) is healed, and therefore our "spirit" or soul, too, is healed.

Because everything is energy, our deciding to, and living a happy, healthier life vibrates out, and on some level, affects others in positive ways. Once you make a conscious decision to free yourself (or heal) your soul, everything else begins to heal and work as it was meant to, in perfection and abundance.

Spiritual Liberation

In essence, healing your soul, and therefore your mind and body so that you can do Highest good, or live a happier, prosperous, and healthier life, paying it forward to others if possible, allows for your "spiritual liberation". What this means is breaking free of the hindrances that heretofore were preventing you from living life to the fullest, another reason you have incarnated here on earth, results through the Mind-Treatments. I will elaborate on this in the next chapter.

The Physical

When you are made aware of an illness, ache, pain, disease in your body, it is a signal that somewhere within your holistic-system, that you have neglected something. It is important, therefore, that like a car, you must physically-fuel your body in healthy ways: hydrate (drink lots of fluids, particularly water), eat whole living foods (organically-grown), and exercise your physical-body regularly; this does not necessarily mean the physically-strenuous exercises of western society, which focuses on the resulting physical beauty of your body, but more so the overall wellness on all levels. Yoga, Tai chi, and Qi Gong are incredible complete health-systems within themselves, and do not require that you strain, tax, or tear anything. It has been scientifically-proven that weight-loss occurs in practitioners of the aforementioned disciplines, simply because one becomes healthy mind, body, and soul with their practice. Blood-pressure is lowered, and the chemistry and physiology of your body becomes balanced.

You can see, then, that working on the health of your soul and mind through the Mind-Treatments must be complimented with the healthy, physical-fuelling of your body through proper diet and exercise.

If you have not been neglecting your physical body in this way (diet and exercise), but are still physically unwell, the answer is in the Mind-Treatments. An emotional trauma (perhaps several) is still lingering within your soul, which must be healed, or your emotional/mental, and therefore physical well-being will be compromised. Phineas Parkhurst Quimby helped many to be healed of physical ailments because the root-cause of their illness was not physical, but that of the soul. Working through their mind as previously described, cured their physical ailments in all cases. I highly recommend you explore his hundreds of documented cases for further proof here: http://www.ppquimby.com/hdresser/manscpts/manscpt.htm

▼

Spiritual Health

Just like physical well-being, spiritual well-being is tied into the holistic-chain of mind/body/soul. If you feel physically-well, your "spirit" (or soul) is happy, and your mind/emotional well-being is at ease. Conversely, if you feel, or are physically unwell, your "spirits" are down, and so is your emotional well-being. If your "spirits" or emotional well-being is down, you are likely physically unwell (either becoming or already feeling physically unwell), and your mind/soul needs healing to fix all.

Freeing/Maintaining/Healing the Spirit

As alluded to in the previous chapter, "Spiritual Liberation" will allow you to lead life to the fullest: happy, healthy, and prosperous. But healing your soul through the Mind-Treatments won't be enough to maintain its good health, and therefore the health of your mind and body.

Seven Spiritual Practices

The "Seven Spiritual Practices", taught by the Agape International Spiritual Center, is most crucial for maintaining one's spiritual health and well-being.

Briefly, they are "Meditation", "Positive Affirmations", "Life-Visioning" TM (a creation of Dr. Michael Beckwith's), "Spiritual Study", "Sacred Service", "Spiritual Community", and "Tithing". I highly recommend you study these through Agape: http://www.agapelive.com/

The practice of these will increase the quality of your life, allowing you to maintain spiritual well-being. The combined practice of these, along with Mind-Treatments to eliminate any hindrances/traumas in your personal subconscious, will eventually allow you a "spiritual liberation".

The Mind-Treatments are simply not enough for the health and healing of your spirit/soul, just as they are not enough for the health and well-being of your physical body. Just like one feeds the "car" or body, one also feeds the soul/spirit via the Seven Spiritual Practices; you are therefore integrating and practicing a truly spiritual life that way.

Recently in my Sunday services, and in my private practice, I have been adding breathing in deep, "Sacred-breath".

Sacred-Breath

Have you ever noticed how naturally you do this throughout your day? You may not even be aware of it; you are busy with some task or tasks, and you let out a "sigh". This is very much like breathing in and releasing the sacred-breath. Notice how calm, relaxed, and rejuvenated you feel after you do this.

Let's stop for a moment now and do this together.

Take in a deep, sacred breath now, and release it with an "ahhhh". Again. Ahhhhhhhhhhh. Feel the Presence. Feel the gratitude for being alive. Let's do it again: take a great deep breath in, and release. "Ahhhhhhhhh". Make your own sacred-sound as you do this, now…maybe "ohhhhhmmmmm". Life is good.

A clinical explanation for the results of doing this deep sigh is that we oxygenate the blood, cells, and tissues of our body, causing a relaxed and rejuvenated feeling. The spiritual explanation could be that since God/Source is everywhere, including the air that we breathe, taking in an extra breath of "sacred breath", or God, makes us feel good, putting us in touch with all things energetically "High": love, happiness, appreciation, creation, joy, etc.

Truly.

Can you say that you don't feel great after doing this? Do this regularly and feel the Presence, the Power.

Holistic Approach

With the Seven Spiritual Practices, healthy diet and exercise, and Mind-Treatments to heal the soul, therefore the mind, therefore the body, you are well on your way to living a truly holistically-healthy, and prosperous life.

▼

CHAPTER 4

Maintenance: Self-Empowering Tools

We would like to recap at this point, the numerous tools that we've provided for you for self-empowerment, within the pages of this book.

Meditation and the Sacred-Breath

First and foremost is meditation. It is the literal "key to the mind". It is the key to peace and prospering. It is the key to stress-management. It is the key to spiritual wellness and maintenance. It is the key to spiritual transformation, and one of the six keys to spiritual liberation. It is the gateway to your source, to God. It is the key to answers: if you have a question in your life, put yourself into altered-state (self-hypnosis/meditation) until you feel that "lazy feeling" or "peak-point" of meditation; that place where you really don't want to think, but you are "conscious" enough to; then affirm and declare that you already have the answer to what you seek, and it is already materializing in your "Mind of God". Allow; allow for divine-inspiration to seep to the surface now, or just let it go. This letting go at this point will allow the answer to come up when you least expect it, either that "ah-hah!" moment, or Source working through circumstances or people to show you the way. Meditation is that gateway.

You already know how to meditate: sit in quiet contemplation. Have no expectations. Take a deep breath and exhale. Then simply "feel". Feel gratitude. Feel love. Feel appreciation for creativity in your life. This is a way for you to know the "Great I Am": love, all things great, your Higher-Self/ Universal Mind/God-Mind. Then if you wish, look up, with eyelids closed, into the interior-region of your forehead as a focal-point. Count your breaths, without forcing them: on the inhalation, "one", on the exhalation, "two, over and over. If your mind wanders, that's okay...don't scold yourself, merely bring it back to the "one-two, one-two".

You may also meditate "consciously" in your day-to-day living.

Be consciously aware of when you're not feeling good at some point in your day; let's say it's just a feeling; notice it immediately, and sublimate it into God's light, transforming it into gratitude or appreciation. Immediately, upon being aware of the negative-feeling, take a sacred-breath in, and release it with an "ahhh", or sigh. Then feel gratitude. Whatever didn't feel good is now gone. Do the same for people who "rub you the wrong way" or "push your buttons".

If someone is rude to you during the day, take a sacred-breath in, release it, and feel gratitude and appreciation for your experience of this person; because it's an opportunity to bless and heal them. They can obviously use a good blessing or healing. Mentally say "bless you" to them, or better, mentally say "I love you" to them. Take another deep, sacred breath, releasing them to God. Feel the power and the Presence.

Self-Hypnosis and Positive Affirmations

The method for getting into altered-state/self-hypnotic state is the same as under "Meditation and the Sacred-Breath".

When you're at that "peak-point", mentally affirm and declare you are whatever or wherever it is you wish to be in your life.   This adds true power to the affirmation. In this way it is not merely a "New-Age" "Positive Affirmation", but a statement of great power and transformation, because you've put God into it, via the route of self-hypnosis/meditation. Stamp the power of the affirmation with "and so it is, amen!" to add further power. There are numerous examples of affirmations for love, health, prosperity, etc. on the Internet, in books, etc. Pick some that feel right for you, or even better, create your own; allow Source's words to flow through you during this process of affirming.

And remember to take that deep breath in, and release. Ahhhhhhhhh. Change your mind, change your life.

Mind-Treatments

I've already gone into great detail about the procedure for doing Mind-Treatments for others, but it can be more difficult doing them on yourself.

Go into meditative/self-hypnotic/altered-state. Be aware of the peek-point, or point of laziness, and letting go. Mentally affirm and declare/set the intention of God healing any past traumas at all levels of your mind. Perhaps you already know which ones, so start with one. Take a deep breath and release. Feel God's love, and appreciation. You might even see light/color(s) which is a signal to your conscious mind of the Presence. Feeling the Presence is easier. Whichever works for you. Remember and visualize the incident, now. See the people and places vividly. See yourself as you were at the time of the incident, and also "walk into" that time as yourself now. The you of now hugs and supports yourself as you were then, filling the you of now and then with God's healing love and light. Take a deep breath, releasing yourself into God. Ahhhhhhh. Feel appreciation for the incident. It made you the strong person that you are today. Bless and release the others involved, by filling them with the Presence; bless them; forgive them; hug them. Give a group hug: see yourself now, hugging yourself then and the others involved with a great big embrace. See all of you filled inside and out with God's light and love and appreciation. See yourselves enveloped inside and out with this light. When you forgive, the healing begins.

Mentally say goodbye to everyone, seeing everyone (including yourself then) as beings of light/God. Take another breath and release. Ahhhhhhhhhh. It feels great. Mentally affirm and declare the healing that occurred, give thanks for it, and end with "and so it is, amen!" Slowly return your senses to the exterior-world once again. Take one more breath and release, and feel the Presence. Feel appreciation.

Remember

Remember to learn and practice the Seven Spiritual Practices from Agape. They, along with the Mind-Treatments, will help you to achieve spiritual liberation.

PART 5-

CASE-HISTORIES

I would like to share with you, at this point, some cases from my case-files of Mind-Treatments. The names, sexes, and occupations/lifestyles of the patients have been changed to keep their anonymity.

Anna and Her Cough

Anna was an unemployed, single, 50-something female. She was divorced thirteen years, and two of her three grown sons lived with her. They were 28 and 30, single, hard-working men. They lived with their mother out of a mutual desire for everyone to do well in life. They were all supportive of each other, with no obvious dysfunctional behaviors.

Anna came to me because she believed she was depressed. She was diagnosed several years ago with clinical depression, and medication was also prescribed for her. I could see a genuine desire in her eyes to rid herself of her so-called depression. Oddly enough, I didn't believe she was depressed. She was somewhat lacking in self-esteem, and had a persistent cough, but she wasn't, in my professional opinion, depressed. I immediately told her this.

"You're not depressed!" I exclaimed, and her eyes lit up. "You know what? I thought not!" was her response. "In fact, I stopped taking my meds three years ago, and I've been feeling even better!" she added. Her posture changed to that reflecting more self-confidence.

"Then you won't need my help?" I quipped. I was feeling her out for a response.

"Well, I just want to make sure," was her answer. This confirmed that she was well enough for us to explore other avenues of therapy and analysis. She also let me know that she had her cough for a few years, and wanted to find out why, and how to be rid of it. I suspected that the appearance of the cough coincided with the willing disappearance of her medication. I had to find out for sure.

Luckily, Anna herself was an Alternative-Wellness Practitioner, so she was comfortable with the prospect of the Mind-Treatments.

During the intake, I learned that like many, her self-esteem dropped after she divorced, and that the whole reason for the divorce, as well as the fear of poverty as a result of divorcing, was still evident 13 years later. Yet she was thriving with her two loving sons. She was still mentally living in the trauma of the past, thus hindering her professional progress: she had stopped practicing her complimentary-medicine, which is what she was born to do.

We began the journey. Fortunately, she also had some previous experience meditating, so it wasn't difficult for her to go into an altered-state. I reinforced Source as her protector, she saw God as the color blue, vividly glowing outward from within herself. Slowly, in her mind, we went back to the time when her husband demanded a divorce, apparently suddenly and unexpectedly. I had the Anna of now support and comfort the Anna of then. The blue light of God enveloping everyone, she blessed and forgave everyone involved, including the catalyst for this all, the "other" woman! Everyone hugged and cried, again, enveloped in God's healing light. She had healed the trauma of 13 years previous, and regained her confidence as an Alternative Wellness Practitioner. However, her cough was still present.

In another session, we dealt with the cough. Getting her into altered-state, I proceeded to help her to substitute self-love for the medication! Rather than the cough, she now had a greater appreciation of herself and her qualities as a person. She no longer relied on her cough, but rather, love of herself.

The trauma of dropping her medication was healed, with self-love instead of a cough remaining.

Albert and the Youthful Heart-Ache

Albert was a successful, 30-something professional, married for eight years, with two young children. His wife was also a working professional, and they both lived in a large, modern house in an affluent part of town. To see Albert, you would never know that a hurt from unrequited love when he was four still haunted him.

He came to me one day, not understanding why he was so unhappy, after all, he had everything. "It is usually rooted in some kind of childhood trauma", I stated, "often abusive parents, or cruel siblings; something of that nature." He thought for a moment, remembering.

He started to tear up. "It was Ginette." I asked him if Ginette was his wife. "No", he declared, "Ginette was someone I loved when I was four." I asked him to share the incident with me. I learned that it was a school-yard rejection of professed love; Ginette cruelly laughed at Albert, saying she could never love someone like him. This stayed with him into adulthood, never allowing Albert to completely be his true, happy, and successful self. It even resulted in him drawing to himself numerous relationships where the woman would ultimately reject him; the vibration of self-rejection kept drawing like a magnet to him those who would reject him. "Like attracts like". I asked him if he was ready to jump off the merry-go-round and move forward; to truly grow forward. He said yes.

Fortunately, Albert was a regular meditator, so going into an altered-state was easy for him. I established God as his protector, and he saw his Source as a gold-light, glowing out from inside of him, surrounding him in an aura of pure, Love-light. Then, we began the journey in his mind, back in time to when he was four.

He saw himself now, approaching the Albert of then, just as the four-year-old Albert was about to declare his love for the potential school-yard sweetheart. I had the Albert of now stand in a supportive-manner of young Albert, holding his shoulders, as the younger Albert received the rejection. I had Albert of now see the gold-light of God embrace young Albert from the inside out, loving and cleansing him of all sorrow. Albert of now wept. They were tears of strength, of love. I asked him how he felt, and he stated "I am grateful". He continued, "Grateful that I met Ginette, grateful that I could feel love and to share that feeling with her. It has made me the loving, compassionate, and sensitive person I am today."

I had Albert of now surround himself, young Albert, and Ginette with loving, healing god-light as they all embraced.

I then had Albert start to return to the present time, strong with self-love, and the strength of Source's eternal light.

Doug's Sister

Doug came to me one day, in an effort to heal from the recent loss of his sister. Mind-Treatments would not usually be used in a situation like this, unless the death held back the patient from being all they can be.

I asked Doug how is life was going: was he happy? Achieving goals? He replied in the affirmative, but when I asked how love was going, he stated that he was divorced, with no plans to date or re-marry. This felt wrong. Why would someone choose to not be in a relationship, short or long-term, unless something traumatic was holding them back? Through further probing, I learned that Doug lack of desire for a relationship didn't start when he divorced, but upon the death of his sister. His mother was still alive, but the loss of his sister, another strong, loving female-figure in his life, had created a fear of losing any other loved women. Hence, he acquired an avoidance of relationships. A perfect jumping-off point for a Mind-Treatment. This illustrates why it is so imperative to determine the root-cause of unwanted behavior/feelings.

I guided Doug to a semi-altered state, helping him to understand that by his sister dying, she did not betray him, or leave him because she did not love him, which is what he believed. I created a dialogue in Doug's mind, between himself and his sister, first establishing the existence/presence of the Presence, or God; I insured that Doug could clearly and powerfully feel and see what he perceived as his creator. Doug saw a bright, purple-light emanating from his chest, and extending ad-infinitum in all directions outward. He felt love and appreciation from deep within this light; I then knew that this link between "God" and Doug was established. Doug would need this strength from God in order to forgive and heal his sister (which we did), and then himself, which we also did. I succeeded in substituting God's eternal Love, Light, Forgiveness, and Gratitude for the loss and betrayal by his sister. I further reinforced this strength by having Doug remember the purple-light and feelings associated with it whenever he felt he needed to.

In short time, Doug was open to the idea of dating again, perhaps even open to marriage one day.

The Over-Weight Model

Sandra was a tall, attractive, 50-something former model. A professional consultant, and mother of two teenagers, Sandra was unhappy with her weight, and came to me asking if Mind-Treatments could help with this. At that point, I recognized that the root-cause of her weight gain had to be uncovered. Usually it would be low self-esteem, or an unconscious desire to protect oneself from life. But intuitively I felt this wasn't the case.

I probed and discovered that one of Sandra's early role-models was her European grandmother. This grandmother regularly insisted that if you weren't fat, you were unhealthy. She continuously established in Sandra's mind a link between being over-weight, and success. This is what needed to shift in Sandra's mind.

Sandra, too, was familiar with altered-states, and easily and willingly went to the centre and nucleus of her mind, where Source resided. She could see God as a blue light, and with a deep breath and release, felt the love and gratitude associated with this blue-light. I established in her mind that nothing was stronger than this, and as she stared deeply into my eyes, focusing on her breathing and the blue-light, she whole-heartedly agreed that only God's strength was real. The concept, I continued, of being fat, didn't mean success, or even good health for that matter. I proceeded to have her associate being over-weight with having ill-health, having her "see" the fatty, cholesterol-filled arteries of a fat person, and compare it with God's strengths of success, love, appreciation, creativity, success, and happiness. I asked her to choose one or the other, and the choice was quick and clear. I had her "see" herself losing weight, becoming more and more healthy, more and more successful and happy, and all she had to do was to take a deep breath in, feeling God's love and appreciation, also seeing the beauty of God's blue-light. I had her see God's blue-light resonating within and around her, creating more and more love and success. Having her take one more deep breath and releasing, we began to conclude the session with having her return her senses to the exterior-world again.

She said that she would never gain weight again.

Part 6-

Summary/Conclusion

Keep in mind that passion and sincere desire to succeed cannot substitute for education and experience. Although I might make the process of the Mind-Treatments sound simple, they are still challenging, even for someone like me who has 15 years experience, with thirty years in total in the metaphysical realm.

The case-histories I described were successful mainly because of God's guidance. I cannot emphasize this enough. It wasn't my human-mind that did the treatment, but the God-part of my mind guiding me with what to say during the treatment. But my allowing of this intuiting-process only began once I felt I had enough practical Hypnotherapy experience. This knowing allows me to relax enough for the words to just flow through me. This cannot be taught in a book. It is a "letting go, and letting God" process.

Often during the intake, if I'm having difficulty in uncovering a root-cause of the illness, I rely on this intuitive-process: the correct words and questioning seems to flow through me, in order to accomplish this. This too, cannot be explained or taught. But it can be acquired.

Acquiring Intuition

As with everything else thus far, even your intuitive senses may be honed via meditation. The more you meditate, the more you will train your human-mind to step back, allowing divine-intuition/guidance to step forward, and up to the surface. Care and attention to your true motivation must be established at this point: do you want to meditate to become more psychic, or for more Divine-contact and higher Intuition? This is the difference between a Psychic and a Healer; a Mystic and a Psychic. The Psychic is more concerned with short-term, band-aid superficial solutions, as opposed to the long-term root-causes and permanent solutions of the Mystic/Healer who wishes to make divine-contact and therefore understand the true nature of the problem, leading to long-term, more permanent solutions. The Mystic may often be Psychic, but a Psychic isn't always a Mystic or Healer.

If the primary goal of meditating is spiritual liberation and enlightenment, then psychic abilities will only be a consequence of the journey, merely one small step, or rung, along the ladder up towards true spirituality. If one stays fixated on just the one rung, then one's spiritual growth becomes stunted.

Choose meditation for spiritual growth. Your intuition will grow naturally that way.

Unrealistic Expectations

In my practice, I constantly hear potential students ask me if I can teach them to do channeling and/or mediumship; to be able to see their aura; to be able to see their angels or spirit-guides; to "make them" more psychic!

There are even those who claim that they can help others to do these things. They establish workshops, and ongoing classes for this purpose. Thus far, I have encountered only well-meaning people doing these workshops. I suspect that there are also less-than-honest people out there doing similar workshops. There was a time when I held regular workshops, written a book, and produced a DVD called "Developing Your Psychic Awareness". My intentions were to help to guide those sincere students, who desired to use their finely-honed intuitive and psychic abilities to help others. I believe I was successful in this regard. Every one of these students desired to help others; they weren't even concerned with themselves as much as with helping others! These were the ones who became my students and went on to become successful, ethical Alternative-Wellness Practitioners, therapists, etc. They had meditation as their base. They had God as their strength. They passed this on.

You Never Really Know

You never really know where life, or your Higher Self, will lead you!

I never suspected while growing up in one of North America's largest bustling metropolises, that by the time I would be in my 50's I would be residing in a smaller, slower-moving, west-coast city, working with people's minds to heal them of whatever ails them.

When I was in my 20's, graduated from Graphic Design in Montreal, my drive and ambition (or Higher-Self?) pushed me to accomplish things that most 20-year-olds don't: I had advertising-art clients based in New York, Paris, and Montreal (Toronto in the '70's was still the same size that Vancouver is today); I was drawing a nationally-syndicated comic-strip, which was my life-long ambition, accomplished by the age of 23! I was also drawing political and gag cartoons that appeared simultaneously in Montreal, Toronto, and Winnipeg. By the time I was 29, I was writing, producing, and starring in a television-show (apparently the longest-running/regularly-produced show in history about magic) until I was 38. I share all of this with you not to brag: I say this first in gratitude, and to also outline the power of passion, about living your dream; about being and living your Authentic-Self, essentially God/Source working through us.

Living Your Dream

This is why we're all here. This is why I do the Mind-Treatments, or Alpha Quantum Therapy © as we also call them, to this day; to enable people to discover their passions/life's purposes, and to do them. You are your Authentic-Self that way; this is how Source/God, etc. works through us. The drive, the passion we have about drawing, or music, or singing, or engineering, or cleaning houses, the drive that is too great for us to stop it, is what I'm encouraging in others. Creativity *is* Creation/Creator/Source/God! Why stop it from coming through us?

Fear, self-doubt stops this drive.

Everyone deserves to do their passion, their heart's desire. If you think you can't, this is why I am here. To help you (which is the same as helping myself, since we are all One) on your spiritual journey; to help you to spiritually liberate yourself!

I understand how it feels to just know that "you can do anything you want, be anything you please" (which, by the way, was the name of the theme-song to my TV-show, and what we sing Sunday-mornings at my New Thought ministry). This is why I had the wondrous, blessed experiences in the first half of my life, in the eastern cities of Canada. So that I can honestly say that it's been proven to me; I can truly say that passion+drive+action+belief=success/God in action!

Afterword

Now you understand.

You understand that you already have the key to wellness, to love, money, joy, abundance, and prosperity.

The key is accessing, through meditation, that which is the Source of us all, which resides within each and every one of us. The more you experience Source-energy via meditation, the freer and happier you will feel. The happier you will feel, the more you will resonate to the same vibrations as abundance and the endless source of that which we are from. This allowing will cause creative ideas to come to you, for acquiring that which you desire. You need merely step out of your own way and allow abundance to flow to you. Allow by being joyous and happy. Take a deep breath of Sacred-Breath, and release. Spiritually liberate yourself; free/allow Source to work miracles through you; allow Source to create through you.

The possibilities are endless.

Via the Mind-Treatments/Alpha Quantum Therapy© you can heal yourself and others; removing negativity; removing emotional traumas which created emotional despair, and thus caused you to hinder your own progress, your own creative output. It's time to take responsibility for your own spiritual liberation.

Your own mind is the key, for deep within it lies those hindrances, those traumas, just waiting to be loved, just waiting to be healed by Source's joy, Source's eternal, endless abundance and creativity.

A quick word about "Alpha Quantum Therapy©", or rather the origins of the name.

A friend of mine had suggested that some people don't feel comfortable with the name "Mind-Treatments", which suggests, inaccurately, a manipulation of the mind; furthermore she suggested that some people also don't feel comfortable with the word "hypnotherapy", again for the same reason. She felt that some would feel more comfortable with the softer word "Therapy", and "Quantum", since the popularity of "Quantum Physics". I liked the more clinically-accurate description of the Mind-Treatments as "Quantum-Therapy", (as she originally suggested) since in Quantum Physics, the "Universal Mind", (as it is called in New Thought philosophy/Spiritual Science) or "God"/"Source" in theology, is sometimes referred-to as the "Divine-Matrix", suggesting that we exist inside and around a God/Divine-matrix, and it exists inside and around us; hence a salute to Quantum Physics' "Divine-Matrix" with the usage of the word "Quantum" in the name. "Alpha" is the brainwave-state the patient enters into during the treatment, hence the alternate name for the Mind-Treatments, "Alpha Quantum Therapy"© was born.

Take the information contained within this book, and use it (as it was intended) to be historical reference, spiritual, philosophical, and psychological reference and information, and most importantly, as reference-material for the crucial steps towards spiritual liberation: freeing yourself of any self-doubt, leading to ultimate happiness and a greater quality of life.

May You Always allow God to Guide You,

Blessings,
Rev. Dr. Michael H. Likey
Coquitlam, Canada.

About The Author

Rev. Dr. Michael Likey is an Ordained Metaphysical/New Thought Minister through the International Metaphysical Ministry (U.S.A.). He is also a certified Clinical Hypnotherapist, having graduated through the Robert Shields College (England) and earned his double-Doctorate through Dr. Paul Leon Masters' University of Metaphysics/University of Sedona (U.S.A.). He is also a Certified Reiki-Master (through Susan Fisch, Canada). He is a Member of the Association of Ethical and Professional Hypnotherapists, (England) Member of the American Metaphysical Doctors Association, and also Associate-Member of the Canadian International Metaphysical Ministry. He is the author of numerous self-help and metaphysical books, and his exclusive line of DVDs and CDs often sell out. Currently, Michael publishes an online newsletter which he distributes to his clients, tours with his Inspirational Speaking concerts and workshops, has his own Ministry, "Michael's International Spiritual-Light Centre", and enjoys a private Metaphysical practice on the beautiful west-coast of Canada, where he resides with his wife Susan, and their cat Bella. Learn more here:

http://michaellikey.tripod.com/michaellikey

Resources

Elias, Jack 2006
FINDING TRUE MAGIC. Seattle, Washington:
Five Wisdoms Press

Goldberg, Dr. Bruce 2004
NEW AGE HYPNOSIS. St. Paul, Minnesota:
Llewellyn Publications

Grinder, John and Richard Bandler 1981
TRANSFORMATIONS. Moab, Utah:
Real People Press

Hathaway, Michael R. 2003
THE EVERYTHING HYPNOSIS BOOK. Avon, Minnesota:
Adams Media Corporation

Hewitt, William W. 2004
HYPNOSIS FOR BEGINNERS. St. Paul, Minnesota:
Llewellyn Publications

Markham, Ursula 1993
HYPNOSIS. Boston, Massachusetts:
Charles E. Tuttle Company, Inc.

Masters, Dr. Paul Leon 1989
MASTERS DEGREE LEVEL LESSON 2. Sedona, Arizona:
University of Metaphysics

Mishra, Rammurti S. 1987
FUNDAMENTALS OF YOGA. New York, New York:
Harmony Books

Morris, Freda 1975
SELF-HYPNOSIS IN TWO DAYS. Toronto, Ontario:
Clarke, Irwin, & Company, Limited

Newton, Dr. Michael 2004
LIFE BETWEEN LIVES. St. Paul, Minnesota:
Llewellyn Publications

Seale, Ervin 1986
MINGLING MINDS. Harlow, Marina del Rey, California:
DEVORSS Publications

Shields, Robert 2003
HYPNOTHERAPY DIPLOMA COURSE. Harlow, Essex, England:
The Robert Shields College

Slate, Joe H. 2005
BEYOND REINCARNATION. Woodbury, Minnesota:
Llewellyn Publications